"Mikhail Goldis' memoirs, superbly translated by his grandson Marat Grinberg, provide a gripping account of the life of a Jewish prosecutor and detective in the former Soviet Ukraine. Goldis' many insights into the complexity of the Soviet Jewish experience make this book especially rewarding."

—*Samuel D. Kassow,*
*Professor of History, Trinity College*

"Seemingly straightforward and unpretentious, Mikhail Goldis's memoir is packed with intriguing characters, psychological insights, and breathtaking narrative twists. Students of Soviet Ukrainian post-WWII history, Jewish and memory studies and all those who enjoy mystery and suspense won't be able to put this book aside. Kudos to Marat Grinberg on this excellent translation which brings his grandfather's captivating text to the English-speaking audience!"

—*Radislav Lapushin,*
*Associate Professor of Russian*
*at the University of North Carolina at Chapel Hill*

"Among the growing number of memoirs and documents of post-WWII Soviet Jewish life available in English, few approach the liveliness, nuance, and novelistic suspense of Mikhail Goldis's Memoirs of a Jewish District Attorney from Soviet Ukraine. Elegantly translated, edited, and introduced by Marat Grinberg, Goldis's grandson and one of the leading scholars of Soviet Jewry, the book offers not only sustained sensitive reflections on history, justice, and identity, but also a collection of true crime stories that ought to satisfy the most discerning fans of that genre. Readers will come away with a deeper appreciation of the richly varied, intertwined lives Jews and ethnic Ukrainians led under Soviet rule."

—*Boris Dralyuk,*
*translator of Isaac Babel, Andrey Kurkov,*
*and other authors*

# Memoirs of a Jewish District Attorney from Soviet Ukraine

**Immigrant Worlds & Texts (Series)**
**Series Editor:** Maxim D. Shrayer (Boston College)

**Editorial Board**
Rosana Kohl Bines (Pontifical Catholic University of Rio de Janeiro, Brazil)
Anna Lushenkova Foscolo (Jean Moulin Lyon 3 University, France)
Luis Krausz (University of São Paulo, Brazil)
Boris Lanin (Adam Mickiewicz University, Poland)
Holli Levitsky (Loyola Marymount University, USA)
Hilla Peled-Shapira (Bar-Ilan University, Israel)
Valentina Parisi (University of Macerata, Italy)
Fedor Poljakov (University of Vienna, Austria)
Marco Sabbatini (University of Pisa, Italy)
Mitsunori Sagae (Soka University, Japan)
Franck Salameh (Boston College, USA)
Hana Wirth-Nesher (Tel Aviv University)

# Memoirs of a Jewish District Attorney from Soviet Ukraine

Mikhail Goldis

Translated, Edited, and with an Introduction by Marat Grinberg

ACADEMIC STUDIES PRESS
BOSTON
2024

Marat Grinberg thanks Reed College's Summer scholarship fund for assisting with the publication of this book. The editor of the book series, Maxim D. Shrayer, thanks Boston College for providing support for the publication of this book.

Library of Congress Cataloging-in-Publication Data

Names: Goldis, Mikhail, author. | Grinberg, Marat, 1977—translator.
Title: Memoirs of a Jewish district attorney from Soviet Ukraine / Mikhail Goldis ; translated, edited, and with an introduction by Marat Grinberg.
Description: Boston : Academic Studies Press, 2024. | Series: Immigrant worlds & texts | Includes bibliographical references.
Identifiers: LCCN 2024020428 (print) | LCCN 2024020429 (ebook) | ISBN 9798887195896 (hardback) | ISBN 9798887195902 (paperback) | ISBN 9798887195919 (adobe pdf) | ISBN 9798887195926 (epub)
Subjects: LCSH: Goldis, Mikhail. | Jewish lawyers—Ukraine—Biography. |
Public prosecutors—Ukraine—Biography. | Public prosecutors—Ukraine—History—Sources. | Ukraine—Politics and government—1921–1944. | Ukraine—Politics and government—1945–1991.
Classification: LCC KLP110.G65 G65 2024 (print) | LCC KLP110.G65 (ebook) | DDC 340.092 [B]—dc23/20240509
LC record available at https://lccn.loc.gov/2024020428
LC ebook record available at https://lccn.loc.gov/2024020429

Copyright © Marat Grinberg, 2024

Book design by Tatiana Vernikov
Cover design by Ivan Grave

Published by Academic Studies Press
1007 Chestnut St.
Newton, MA 02464, USA
press@academicstudiespress.com
www.academicstudiespress.com

*To the blessed memory
of* **Hirsh**, **Sofia**, *and* **Tunya Shichman**,
*murdered by the Nazis and their collaborators
in Belendiika, Ukraine on September 17, 1941.*

# Contents

| | |
|---|---|
| Introduction | ix |

### Part One: Criminal Cases

**The Krasyliv Years**

| | |
|---|---|
| 1. A Jewish Hullabaloo | 3 |
| 2. Thou Shalt Not Kill | 10 |
| 3. Meir and Khoma | 16 |
| 4. Guilty without Guilt | 22 |
| 5. On the Shores of the River Bug | 28 |

**The Kamyanets-Podilskyi Years**

| | |
|---|---|
| 6. The Forbidden Zone | 49 |
| 7. "Seven Forty" | 58 |
| 8. A Mistaken Object | 63 |
| 9. Twenty Years Later | 70 |
| 10. A Defendant's Oral Argument | 79 |

**Women**

| | |
|---|---|
| 11. Valya-Valentina | 88 |
| 12. Samara | 95 |
| 13. Nadezhda Petrovna | 103 |
| 14. Alla | 109 |

### Part Two: Other Memoirs

| | |
|---|---|
| 15. Serbiyanka | 116 |
| 16. Above the Abyss | 131 |
| 17. One Day in the Life of a Detective | 137 |
| Notes | 145 |

# Introduction

One of my earliest childhood memories is of my grandfather, Mikhail Goldis, in the kitchen of his apartment in Khmelnytskyi, Ukraine, a cigarette in hand, talking about cases at work, some recent and some that took place a while back. A cigarette would disappear—he quit smoking in his early '60s—but everything else continued, with new details added, graphic, psychological, and political, which I, now a teenager or an adult, could grasp and appreciate to a much fuller extent. When we immigrated to the US in 1993, my grandfather was sixty-seven years old, energetic, robust, and willing to adjust to the new country and life. This was, of course, hardly an easy process—the pain of immigration is always real—which is why, I think, he decided, with the encouragement of my grandmother, Maya Moshchinskaya, to start putting his memories and experiences on paper. A superb oral storyteller and an avid reader of literature, he loved the process of writing and editing and kept on turning out piece after piece. The writing, at times therapeutic and at times traumatic, activated the creative streak he always possessed, allowing him to produce a narrative of his life and via it of postwar Soviet Ukraine, and what it took for a Jewish attorney to survive in the halls of Soviet power. The stories, *rasskazy* as he called them, were first serialized in the Russian-language magazine *Zerkalo* (Mirror) from

1995-2003, published in the Twin Cities, where he lived, and then came out as a separate book in 2013.[1] In the last few years of his life, he was working on a new set of memoirs, largely personal episodes and family histories, which remained unfinished. Translating, editing, and researching the published memoirs allowed me to reengage with their content and rediscover it as a multifaceted cultural and historical document, a testimony both to its time and the complexities of human character. The Soviet, Russian, Ukrainian, and Jewish components are intertwined in it with deeply nuanced reflections on human nature in its worst and best manifestations, something Goldis learned both from his career and life, as well as from his favorite authors, Chekhov and Tolstoy, Viktor Nekrasov, and Vasily Grossman.

Goldis with his grandson, Marat Grinberg,
Kamyanets-Podilskyi, Ukraine, 1978.

Introduction | XI

Goldis writing his memoirs in his apartment in St. Paul, Minnesota, late 1990s.

\*\*\*

Mikhail Goldis was born on July 13, 1926 in the small town of Yaltushkiv in the Bar district of the Vinnytsia region in Ukraine. Prior to Soviet rule, it was a shtetl; by the start of World War II and the German occupation, Jews still constituted half of Yaltushkiv's population. A renowned Chasidic tsadik and one of the disciples of Baal Shem-Tov, Yehuda Leib Sarah (1730-1796), is buried there. Goldis was a twin; his sister, Mila, died at the age of six from scarlet fever. In 1931, his sister Nella was born, an important and beloved person in Goldis's life. She would go on to become a teacher of history and live most of her life in Vinnytsia. She immigrated to the US in 1999 and died in 2017 in Minneapolis.

Mikhail was born to Leah (later she russified the name to Elizaveta) Shichman (1908-1971) and Bentsion Goldis (1900-1943), whose backgrounds were both different and alike. Bentsion came from an incredibly poor family; he was a self-made man with no education. He started to work when he was ten, becoming the manager of a sugar plant in the

Mikhail Goldis and his twin sister, Mila, circa 1928.

Vinnytsia region just eighteen years down the road. This was an important and influential regional post. In 1937, at the peak of Stalin's terror, he was fired from his position while his party membership was revoked; the pretext seems to have been a joke he told about Stalin. By some miracle, he was not arrested and he soon had his party membership and job reinstated. He perished in 1943 in the battles for the liberation of Kyiv. In the letters he wrote to his son from the front, he talked about the incredible pride he had in the Soviet state which had enabled him, an uneducated poor nobody, to truly become a somebody. All his extended family, including his mother, were murdered by the Nazis in Yaltushkiv. His father was killed earlier in a pogrom, perpetrated by Ukrainian insurgents led by Symon Petlyura during the civil war.

Unlike the Goldises, Leah's family were members of intelligentsia. Her father, Hirsh (she russified her patronymic to

Goldis's father, Bentsion, at the front, circa 1942.

Grigorievna), was a teacher of Russian language and literature in Haysin, a larger town and an important Jewish center in the Vinnytsia region. He and his wife, Sofia, took an active part in raising the young Misha and were instrumental in inculcating in him a love for reading and knowledge. Hirsh, Sofia, and their younger daughter, Misha's aunt Tunya, were murdered, along with the other Jews from the area, on a farm near Haysin, called Belendiika, in 1941 by the Nazis. My grandfather carried a deep trauma and guilt over their death throughout his life and would have been heartened to see that I have dedicated this book to their memory. After the war, Leah, who was now Liza, continued to work at the sugar plant. She died in Vinnytsia in 1971. Goldis revered his mother and was devastated by her early death.

The four elements—Soviet, Russian, Ukrainian, and Jewish—coalesced in Goldis's childhood and youth in ways that were typical for his generation, but at the same time quite unique. Both party members, the parents were genuinely dedicated to the Soviet cause, and while they continued to speak Yiddish, at least in private, they rebelled against everything that had to with Judaism and the traditional way of life. They named their son Mikhail in honor of Mikhail Frunze, a Bolshevik civil war hero. As a youngster, a red kerchief on her head, Leah would walk through her neighborhood on Yom Kippur waving a pork sausage in protest.

My grandfather recalled how his grandmother on his father's side, who spoke no Russian, would lock herself up in a room in their house on Saturdays and mumble her prayers there. Such stories are well known to students of early Soviet Jewish life in the former Pale of Settlement. The unusual element came from growing up at a sugar plant in Yaltushkiv and then in Haysin, which constituted a small town of its own and had hardly any Jews. Because of this, and unlike the great majority of Soviet Ukrainian Jews of his generation, Goldis knew not a single word of Yiddish (he would later acquire a few juicy terms and expressions and sprinkle his speech with them), but was intimately familiar with Ukrainian rural life, its language and mores, which proved to be of great importance during his career as a detective and district attorney. Always coexisting with this, however, was his distinct and deeply entrenched Jewish self-awareness and a sense of spirituality—not, unsurprisingly, in any observant sense.

The story of his evacuation with his mother and little sister to the Saratov region at the start of the war and his subsequent military conscription is told vividly and powerfully in the chapter "Serbiyanka," so I won't dwell on it here; but I would like to add a few noteworthy details. At the front, Goldis was a signalman; a junior lieutenant and a commander of a rifle platoon. He was wounded on September 9, 1944 in a battle near the Lithuanian city of Siauliai, and shrapnel from the bullet remained in his left shoulder for the rest of his life. It was in the field hospital where he was recovering from the wound that his first vivid encounter with antisemitism took place. He loved to sing, was good at it, and one day joined in with his fellow soldiers who were humming Russian and Ukrainian folk songs. A nurse, sitting nearby, told him to stop and added, "You cannot be singing our songs. You're a Jew." Other Soviet Jewish memoirists echo how the ubiquity of antisemitism in the Red Army during the war became their crucible moment.

At that point, Goldis also lost any contact with his mother and sister and was convinced that they were dead, while they thought that he'd been killed or had "disappeared without

Junior Lieutenant Mikhail Goldis at the end of the war.

Goldis with his mother Leah (Elizaveta) on the right and sister Nella on the left, circa 1948, Sobolivka, Ukraine.

a trace," to use the euphemistic wartime Soviet language. In his discharge documents from the hospital, he indicated that he had no living relatives and put "Russian" for his ethnicity—a subconscious sign of a bitter break with his past. The nurse, or perhaps doctor, to whom he handed the documents asked whether he was indeed Russian. He answered that he was a Jew; she reprimanded him, said that it was wrong to be ashamed of one's people, and told to correct it—which he did. Thus, the war years reaffirmed his sense of Jewishness and made him proud of his identity, while at the same time exposing him to the hate it provokes and the trauma and pain that accompanies it. Goldis's relationship to his identity became more intense, and more complex, as he grew older, and it is a running thread in this book.

In 1948, just a few years after returning from the front as a decorated officer, Goldis enrolled in the prestigious Law Faculty of Kyiv's state university. The choice of law was almost accidental, but also intuitively correct. He found great happiness in studying the philosophy of law, ancient Roman law, and Latin (he would later teach me Latin proverbs). One of his favorite professors was a visitor from Moscow, Vladimir S. Pokrovsky, who would begin each lecture on the history of law by writing all the mandated quotes from Stalin and Lenin, Marx and Engels on the blackboard, and then say, "And now we're going to discuss the actually important material." It was also a period, when Goldis read everything he could lay his hands on, especially the Russian classics, trying to fill in the gaps in his education, and got to know the Ukrainian capital. His graduating thesis was on the utopian classic *What Is to Be Done*, by Nikolai Chernyshevsky, which Goldis made a point of writing without referring to any of the hackneyed ideological criticism that was, of course, prescribed.

In his unfinished account of his youth, Goldis wrote: "My student life was filled with joys and levity. By the end, in the early 1950s, it also became saturated with a healthy dose of antisemitism, the vile state antisemitism." I never did learn the full details of what he often referred to as "my university story," and he never managed to write it down, but it's clear that the harassment he suffered at the height of the antisemitic "anticosmopolitan campaign" was severe, and that he was targeted by both the university administration and his fellow students. This persecution, however, seems to have only strengthened his pride in his Jewishness. He never changed his blatantly Jewish patronymic—Bentsionovych—the son of Zion—to anything Russian. It was professor Pokrovsky who again played a role in this. Giving a lecture about Spinoza in the frenzied antisemitic atmosphere of 1949, he referred to the philosopher by his Jewish name Borukh and called him "this great son of

Goldis, a law student at Kyiv State University.

the Jewish people." My grandfather recalled how news of the lecture spread quickly among the city's Jews, many of whom petitioned the university administration to allow them to attend Pokrovsky's lectures.

In 1952, a year before graduating from university, Goldis met his future wife and my grandmother, Maya Moshchinskaya. Maya was born in 1929 in the town of Mohyliv-Podilskyi, in the Vinnytsia region, and spent her childhood in Haysin. Her father, Anisim Moshchinsky (1903-1941), hailed from Odesa and was the editor of the local newspaper in Haysin; he perished at the front in 1941, just two months into the war. Her older brother, Arkady (1925-1943), a talented and aspiring young man, could have avoided the draft because he had a history of polio. Yet, like so many of the finest of his generation, he volunteered, serving at the front as a machine-gunner; he perished in 1943. Both his and his father's graves are unknown. All of Moshchinsky's extended family, including his parents and his sister's family, were killed by the Nazis in 1941

Maya Moshchinskaya with her parents, grandmother, and brother on the eve of the war, Haysin, Ukraine.

in the Pyatnichany Forest on the outskirts of Vinnytsia. Maya's mother, Polina Royter (1901-1966), worked as a librarian after the war and is buried in Kamianets-Podilskyi. She came from a large educated family (her father was a forester), which, she believed, had a tsadik pedigree. During the war, she was evacuated with the children and her mother to Central Asia, where her mother died, and Arkady went to the military academy and then the front. She shared a special bond with her son-in-law; the chapter "One Day in the Life of a Detective" offers a pithy, but loving, tribute to her remarkable character.

When my grandparents met, Maya was a student in the Philology Faculty of the Vinnytsia pedagogy institute. Her love of books was infectious and her knowledge of literature was vast, and she poured her passion into a teaching career of almost forty years. She discovered Dostoevsky's novels—he was at that time a banned author, essentially—when rummaging through the book junkyards in Vinnytsia, and read them all voraciously. Goldis recalled that there was an immediate attraction between them, based, to an extent, on the commonalities of their families and the tragedies and enormous hardships they suffered because of the war. He wrote in an autobiographical fragment, "From the first days of meeting each other, we became like-minded [*edinomyshlenniki*] in everything. We felt close to each other in all respects." They were married on July 5, 1953, soon after Goldis's graduation and exactly four months after Stalin's death. In 1955, their cherished daughter and only child, Tatyana, my future mother, was born. They were together for fifty-four years until Maya's death in 2007 in Minneapolis. Goldis dedicated his book to her, noting:

> My fate was decided the very first time I saw her.... Her part in the publication of my stories is invaluable.... From the first days of writing, Maya became my active and irreplaceable partner.... With her incredible knowledge of Russian language and literature and a God-given pedagogic talent, she would provide treasured advice and criticism. She would always do so delicately and tactfully, sparing my authorial pride.

He outlived her by thirteen years and died on December 19, 2020 in Minneapolis. This book is a testament to both of their lives.[2]

*\*\*\**

Goldis's career in law enforcement as a detective and then a district attorney spanned almost forty years; its vicissitudes, failures, and successes are portrayed in this book. His personality—reserved, self-deprecating, but also incredibly warm,

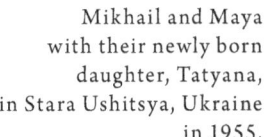
Mikhail and Maya with their newly born daughter, Tatyana, in Stara Ushitsya, Ukraine in 1955.

dignified, and vivacious, with a genuine interest in and love for life—comes through his narrator's voice, which I hope to have captured in English. The book speaks for itself. Here, I would like to briefly pinpoint its interwoven main threads and preoccupations—Soviet, Jewish, Ukrainian, moral, and professional—and why Goldis's perspective as both a witness and a narrator is so significant and singular.

Most of the Jews who went into law in the Soviet Union became defense attorneys, so his choice to enter the prosecuting branch was quite unusual. What attracted him to it? Certainly a pursuit of justice and the thrill of detective work—not a desire to be close to the regime. While the job required joining the Communist Party and serving as state, essentially, Goldis developed from early on a profound skepticism about the authorities and eventually understood that the Soviet system was totally and irredeemably corrupt.

In an unpublished memoir fragment, he recalls a trip to the opera when his then fiancée visited him in Kyiv. Unable to get tickets, they stopped by the backdoor entrance, hoping to sneak in. What they observed was quite extraordinary:

a convoy of luxury automobiles pulled up and a number of party, KGB, and police bosses stepped out. They were greeted by the theater director, who was, of course, wearing black tie. He stood to attention like a young recruit and then bowed to each one of them, making sure that the most important of these members of the political elite got the lowest bow. Goldis writes:

> at this moment, he looked like a mannequin, a clockwork automaton. The entire government flock passed by him in silence, as if he were invisible. Maya and I could not believe our eyes. We thought we got transported back to the Tzarist times. Lermontov's lines about Russia, "the country of slaves, the country of masters . . . ," immediately came to our minds.

The shock of this spectacle stayed with Goldis for the rest of his life. While he valued the attorney job because through it he could combat evil—murder, rape, theft—and put the law to noble use, he always knew that above him there towered a rotten and merciless apparatus that saw him, a Jew, as a second-rate citizen at best. The chapter titled "The Forbidden Zone" provides Goldis's particularly astute assessment of how this system functioned.

Honesty and integrity were the two qualities Goldis most cultivated in himself and praised in others; this meant that he never took bribes and, as a consequence, was considered an oddity in his circles. At the same time, as readers will discover, on the scale between stringency and leniency, he often fell on the side of leniency, which meant he broke the law at times. A brilliant detective who cracked a number of the most intractable and long-standing cases, some of which were overseen by the authorities in Moscow, he was certainly guided by the law,

Goldis giving a lecture, Khmelnytskyi, Ukraine, early 1980s.

but also by the realization that it could not encompass all the complexity of human nature and relationships. What mattered to him were the individuals caught up in life's contingencies. In this respect, he reminds me of Georges Simenon's inspector Maigret or Peter Falk's Columbo. Neither a dissident nor an outright rebel, then, he made bold decisions that could have easily demolished his career. His favorite Russian writers, foremost among them Tolstoy, were partly behind his belief in balancing justice and empathy, and in the chapter "One Day in the Life of a Detective," he remarks on the primacy of empathy: "I thought about how easy it is to humiliate a person, and how little a person needs to feel happy." Indeed, some of the folks Goldis portrays resemble the "little men" in the great Russian novels of the nineteenth century—but transported to the post-Stalinist, post-World War II, and post-Holocaust Ukrainian provinces.

Goldis was always a Jewish insider/outsider within the system. As I said, he was a rarity among Jews in some crucial respects: he didn't know any Yiddish; he was a prosecuting attorney and one of the few who didn't change his Jewish patronymic. At the same time, Goldis was a prototypical member of Soviet Jewish intelligentsia, shaped by what I call in my own research *The Soviet Jewish Bookshelf*.[3] He was an avid reader of Lion Feuchtwanger's historical novels and Sholem Aleichem's *Teye the Milkman*, and saw Anatoly Rybakov's novel *Heavy Sand* as a primer on what it meant to be a Soviet Jew. His memoirs, therefore, are a vivid and rich source on Jewishness in the Soviet Union, including the conspicuousness and utter pervasiveness of antisemitism.

Most valuable, however, is Goldis's own perspective on his Jewish identity. My grandfather was a lover of poetry, from Alexander Pushkin and Nikolai Nekrasov in the nineteenth century, to Sergei Esenin and Marina Tsvetaeva in the twentieth, to Evgeny Evtushenko and Bella Akhmadulina among his contemporaries; of the war poets, he loved Konstantin Simonov in particular, and I spent hours in fierce debates trying to dissuade him of Simonov's worth. In the last years of his life, he developed a special liking for Boris Slutsky, and not only because Slutsky was the main subject of my writing.[4] Two of Slutsky's poems illustrate incisively Goldis's Jewish sensibility. The first is "These Abram, Isak, and Yakov...," which he liked so much that he copied it out on a piece of paper. In the poem, Slutsky plays on the names of the biblical patriarchs in both their scriptural and Russian forms to reveal that while the patriarchs are revered and blessed, the regular Jew "is wretched under any star." The other poem is "To scrawny Jewish children...," in which Slutsky instructs Jewish kids to throw away their chess boards and books and instead take up sports; he does not want them to be afraid of throwing punches, since

Goldis with his World War II regalia in Minneapolis, Minnesota, circa 2018.

"the terrible twentieth century is not over yet." My grandfather admired those Jews who could stand up for themselves—there are a number of them in his memoirs—while never losing sight of Jewish suffering and the constant need for caution. In this respect, his memoirs provide a rare glimpse of how Holocaust memories and stories were guardedly circulated in the Soviet Union, that is, allusively and with omissions.

While Russian language, literature, and culture meant a lot to Goldis, he was, in the final analysis a Ukrainian Jew. He knew Ukrainian provincial and rural life extremely well; he spoke Ukrainian fluently, loved Ukrainian songs and often sang them. The picture of Soviet Ukraine that comes out of these memoirs is not idealized by any means, particularly because he dealt with some of the most vile expressions of human nature, but there are many characters here who are truly noble in spirit—for example, people who risked their lives saving Jews during the war or who spoke the truth in court to their own detriment. Goldis was attached to Ukraine and appreciated its beauty and spirit, but he was also scarred by the scourge and scores of hate directed toward Jews throughout

Mikhail and Maya in Kamyanets-Podilskyi in the courtyard of their apartment. complex on Leningradskaya Street, Kamyanets-Podilskyi, early 1960s.

Ukrainian history and so often in his professional life. Read against the background of the atrocities in Bucha and the still ongoing war, his memoirs are even more poignant and timely. Goldis was outraged when Putin annexed Crimea; he would have been devastated by the events of today and hoped for Ukraine's speedy victory. He would also have been disturbed by the rewriting and whitewashing of some of the darkest and most difficult pages of Ukrainian history.

In translating and editing the memoirs, I divided them into two categories: the largest, which deals with the criminal cases, and the shorter, but striking, "Other Memoirs." The criminal cases are arranged somewhat loosely into the years when he was a detective in Krasyliv, a small district center in the Khmelnytskyi region, and the later years when he worked as a detective and then a deputy district attorney in Kamyanets-Podilskyi. Interspersed throughout the book are episodes from his first location, a small town Stara Ushitsya in the

Khmelnitskyi region, sometimes called the Ukrainian Atlantis, since it was flooded in the early 1970s during the construction of the hydroelectric station on the Dniester river. The most noteworthy place is the ancient and picturesque Kamyanets-Podilskyi in the Podilia region, a provincial city that became an important cultural and education center after the war. It is also my birthplace. Goldis makes this beautiful and haunting city, sometimes called a "flower in stone" or the Ukrainian Florence, come to life. In the memoirs, there is also a separate section on women which is deeply revealing and surprisingly contemporary in its range of subjects and sensibility.

One final note about terminology. I decided to Americanize various important words, rendering *militsia* as "police," *sledovatel'* as "detective" (rather than "investigator"), *prokuratura* as "attorney's office" (rather than "prosecutor's office"), *rayonnaia* as "district," *gorogdskaia* as "city," *respublikanskaia* as "attorney general," and *oblastnaia* as "region." I know my grandfather would have liked to see his words dressed in American "garb."

Goldis's and Moshchinskaya's grave sites, Adath Chesed Shel Emes Cemetery, Minneapolis, Minnesota.

# Part One

## Criminal Cases

# The Krasyliv Years

# 1. A Jewish Hullabaloo

## Ivan Protsyuk's Gang

These events took place in Ukraine in the Krasyliv district of the Khmelnytskyi region, where I worked as a detective in the district attorney's office. One summer night in 1960, a shot was fired through the window of Weisburd, the director of the animal feed section at the local sugar plant. I drove with some police offers to the scene of the incident, where we discovered a bullet inside the house and a sheet of paper, torn from a lined school notebook, on a windowsill. There was a cryptic note on the paper, written legibly but with misspellings: "Ten thousand you get from the bools you fatten. Don't even think of wiggling yourself out of this. How to pass on the money we'll let you know."

By the standards of the time, when the criminal mayhem of the first postwar years had long dissipated, a crime of this type was extremely daring and cunning. A month later, a second shot was fired through Weisburd's window and a second note was left on the windowsill: "If you agree to give up the money, write an ad in the local newspaper. Then we'll tell you where to bring the dough." We came up with an ad and published it in the paper, but no response was forthcoming. Sometime later, however, a shot was fired through the window of Berman, the director of procurement storage. On this occasion, the note said: "Ten thousand from the fat you get from your storage."

In January 1961, the region's law enforcement branches held their annual meeting to reflect on the results of the past year. In his presiding speech about the role of law enforcement in preparing and carrying out the harvest, the head of the district executive committee mentioned the window incidents.[5] "It's clear that something must be done with this Jewish hullabaloo," he concluded with a slight smile (both Weisburd and Berman were Jewish). The law enforcement operatives held in sighs of relief. If the authorities thought the crimes were merely "Jewish hullabaloo," they wouldn't have to worry too much about finding the culprits.

Less than a month had passed when another shot was fired; this time, though, it wasn't at a Jewish home, but a Ukrainian's—that of the sugar plant's director. And then another, at the district attorney's house, a non-Jew, of course. And once again, the perpetrator left a message: "15 thousand from the bribes you take."

Soon afterwards, the police chief received two letters, each telling him to drop the case. Whoever penned the letters informed him that they were part of a well-organized gang with weapons and transportation. They warned him that if the police continued with their zealous investigation, they and their families would be blown to pieces. Jokes and wry smiles about a Jewish hullabaloo quickly stopped. Everyone was on alert, including the head of the executive committee. No one knew whose window would be next.

The chief of the local department of internal affairs was summoned to the attorney general's headquarters in Kyiv and given two options: either solve the case ASAP or resign. He chose the first—and the investigation started to heat up.

\*\*\*

Forensics discovered that all the bullets were fired from the same rifle. Data was gathered about local crimes involving rifles, and among them was the armed robbery of a house in the village of Kharytonivka in the Dunaivtsi region. The case was still open. Further examination of the evidence concluded that the same rifle was used in both Krasyliv and Kharytonivka. Consequently, our primary attention was directed towards establishing other connections between the crimes, including any postal correspondence between residents of Krasyliv and Kharytonivka. It soon turned out that a woman in Kharytonivka had written to someone in Krasyliv by the name of Ivan Protsyuk, begging him to leave her husband alone. This man, Nikolai, couldn't—and didn't want to—continue associating with Protsyuk, whom he'd known since youth. The woman added that her husband was an elderly and honest man. This letter was in our hands in the summer of 1961.

The criminal siege of Krasyliv, which lasted for a year, was finally broken. Protsyuk was arrested, and his buddies, whom he quickly gave up, soon afterwards. There were three of them: Protsyuk, his nephew Andrei Zaika, well known in Krasyliv as a shady person, and Nikolai Kharkiv, a geography teacher at a village school.

The investigation entered a new and painstaking phase, consisting of identifying a myriad of crimes they'd committed, and gathering and interpreting the evidence. In the last stages of the investigation, a permanent detective-police unit was formed in which I was included. We discovered that Protsyuk was the head of the gang. By the time of his arrest, he had just turned sixty. A stableman at the local kolkhoz (collective farm), he was a married man with children and grandchildren. We could hardly believe that this man had kept us on our toes for a whole year. But when we saw that he was tall, muscular, and strong, our naive assumptions exposed. A criminal mastermind had hidden behind the mask of an elderly, kind-hearted, and uneducated man.

Protsyuk pointed, precisely, to all the places he'd fired at and robbed, and turned in two rifles he tenderly called Katya and Marusya. He admitted that he'd written all the letters himself, which our experts confirmed. He named his companions, Kharkiv and Zaika, who wouldn't confess to anything at first. He started to chatter nonstop.

A life-long criminal, Protsyuk had never been arrested. His was a unique case. He scrupulously described his escapades. He even turned in his former lover, Darya, and her husband, who'd "worked" with him after the war and now lived an honest and peaceful life in Kyiv. When Darya heard how her former admirer had ratted her out and boasted about breaking into homes, brandishing "Katya" and "Marusya" in their arms, she fainted. After regaining consciousness, she told him: "You old fool, who asked you to open your mouth? Who needs to hear about your old adventures?"

Protsyuk provided a political reason for his misdeeds, proclaiming that he was a truer follower of Lenin than any of us. He did what Lenin had taught: he robbed only the rich. During the war, he'd gone after Nazi collaborators; after the war, he'd turned his attention to anyone who'd returned from Germany with wealth; and recently, he'd targeted corrupt officials.

Recording his confessions, sixty volumes in total, took an enormous amount of time and effort. When I asked him why he hadn't carried out any of the threats in his letters, he laughed and assured me that he wasn't motivated by money. He'd just wanted to frighten and blackmail people he believed were crooks.

Finally, everything was complete and signed. Protsyuk took of his glasses and uttered, with satisfaction, in Ukrainian: "Seems like this is it." To his surprise, I replied, "Is it really, Ivan Semenovich?"

### *The War Echo*

Four years prior to the arrest of Protsyuk and his gang, a man by the name of Kholod had disappeared in Krasyliv. An elderly married man and a homeowner, he was respected in town as a hardworking and honest expert on wells. Kholod's sisters informed the district attorney's office of his disappearance. His wife, however, did not seem concerned. She told us that Kholod had a habit of traveling far and wide without letting anyone know beforehand. Yet while she said that he could have gone to Siberia or Moldova, his sisters were convinced that he'd been killed and were inconsolable.

A criminal case was opened, but nothing came of our inquiries. Kholod was nowhere to be found. While investigating Protsyuk, though, we established that Kholod's wife was Protsyuk's sister and that Zaika, his gang associate, was Kholod's stepson. Naturally, we started to suspect that Protsyuk was involved in Kholod's disappearance and likely his murder. The challenge was how to question him without any evidence to hand. Luckily, I formed a good relationship with Protsyuk during the many months of investigating him. As we used to say, there is a contract between the detective and the accused. Still, I hesitated asking him directly: it's one thing to confess to robbery and theft and another to homicide.

I took a risk and asked him: "Is this really it, Ivan Semenovich?" Prostyuk looked at me with surprise. I took a piece of paper, wrote "Kholod" on it, folded it, and handed it to him, saying, "My question to you is written on this piece of paper. Read it when you return to the cell and provide a response tomorrow." Protsyuk agreed. I was just about to call a warden, when I heard his voice: "Why wait till tomorrow—let me take a look now." He unfolded the paper. I watched him and saw that his face was turning red. That wasn't the alarming thing, however. I was more concerned about his silence—innocent men don't clam up. I said: "Ivan Semenovich, you don't need to say anything. You answered my question with your silence."

We lit cigarettes, and then Protsyuk began to tell me about the murder. After yet another robbery, Zaika hid some of the stolen items in Kholod's attic. Kholod found them by accident and threatened to go to the police. Zaika told Protsyuk about what had happened, and they decided to kill Kholod. Protsyuk went to his wife, Kholod's sister, with the news. He argued that it was necessary to sacrifice her brother for the sake of her son and husband; she agreed. That night, Protsyuk strangled the sleeping Kholod with a length of wire. He and Zaika immediately drove the body to an empty field on the outskirts of Krasyliv and buried him there.

The day after Protsyuk admitted to the crime, he took us to the field and we started searching for the body—but we didn't find anything. Most likely, Protsyuk had forgotten where it was, as they'd buried Kholod in an unmarked and featureless area.

Continuing the search the next day, we uncovered multiple human remains. We were dumbfounded. Forensic experts were called in, and they determined that we'd found the remains of children buried approximately twenty years previously. This discovery—that children were massacred in Krasyliv during the war—was added to Protsyuk's file. A few days later, as more facts came to the fore, we learned that these children were shot by the Nazis and Ukrainian collaborators. The children were from mixed Ukrainian-Jewish marriages. Some of their mothers—Ukrainian women—came to see us, testifying how their children were taken away and murdered because their fathers were Jewish.

It was unbearably difficult to listen to them and see their grief; twenty years after this mass murder, we'd unwillingly torn open old wounds. The women were questioned and a special case was opened about the murder of children by the Germans in Krasyliv; the details of the case were forwarded to the regional KGB office for further investigation. The Nazis' accomplices were hunted down, charged, and found guilty. Thus, many years after the end of the war, we heard its sorrowful echo...[6]

## 2. Thou Shalt Not Kill

As a detective in Krasyliv's district attorney's office, I was entitled to a phone at home—a rare privilege at the time. But like many other privileges, I never got one. The system barely worked. Consequently, at night, after work, I'd often be notified of an emergency situation (what was called a "ChePe"—literally an extraordinary occurrence) via a simple but reliable method: a policeman on duty would knock on my window and call out: "Please get up, there's a murder" or "There's been a rape/accident/theft," what have you. I would get up and go out into the night to investigate the next ChePe.

I broke this rule once. Awoken during the night by a siren, I started to get ready, afraid that it meant there'd been a serious crime. Despite my wife's protestations, I went outside and realized that the noise was coming from the direction of the sugar plant—so I headed there. On the way, lots of people ran past me. I hurried, and when I got there, I found a crowd of people and numerous trucks outside—fire, emergency, and police. There couldn't be any doubt that something very serious had just taken place.

The plant director's office was full of people. He invited me in and asked, "Are you from police headquarters?" The question was bizarre, as we knew each other well. "Don't you recognize me?" I asked in irritation. He calmly explained that he recognized me, of course, but wanted to know if I'd come as a member of the citizens' defense brigade—because the plant had been holding air defense exercises that night. I sat there for a short while, out of politeness, and then trudged back home. I should have listened to my wife. After that, I stopped paying attention to the night sirens and waited instead of a knock on the window.

It didn't take long. One autumn night, a policeman woke me up and apprised me of an armed assault on an individual. At the police station, I was given the details, and at 2:00 a.m., a report came in that someone had been admitted to the hospital with a gun wound to his hand. The victim's name was Yuri Vengrenyuk. A twenty-year-old guy, whose father had tried to shield him from justice a number times, he was well-known for his criminal behavior. Now this Vengrenyuk was himself the victim of a serious crime.

I questioned him at the hospital. Squirming in pain, he told me that, passing through a school grounds after midnight, he was approached by three men who demanded his money. Then he heard a shot and felt a burning in his hand. Vengrenyuk described the culprits—height, age, hair color, clothes, and so on. The forensic examination concluded that the shot came from a hunting rifle.

At ten o'clock in the morning, tired and starving police detectives and I were sitting in the chief of police's office coming up with and discussing various theories about what might have happened. A policeman knocked on the door and informed the chief that a local priest wanted to see him. Annoyed, the chief asked to let the priest know that he was extremely busy and would not be able to receive him today. Five to ten minutes later, the same policeman—this time red-faced—knocked again and told us that the priest wouldn't leave and was insisting that they meet straightaway. The chief acquiesced, let the priest come into his office, and told him to be as brief as possible; we were, after all, trying to solve a serious crime. The priest nodded and said: "The thing is, my dear sirs, that I either killed or wounded a man tonight." He then proceeded to recount the events.

That night, the priest had been woken by a commotion coming from the room in his house in which he kept his liturgical objects. Hearing men's voices and the clatter of items being thrown around, he realized there were thieves in the house. He took his hunting rifle and stood by the door which led to the hallway. The thieves were trying to open it. He decided to scare them off and fired through the door. There was a loud scream, followed by silence. The priest knew that he'd hit one of the men and possibly killed him.

Had a hidden camera filmed our drawn faces and gaping mouths, it would've looked like something out of the end of Gogol's *Inspector General*.[7] It took me a couple of minutes to snap out of my stupor. I then called the hospital and ordered Vengrenyuk's transfer to a preliminary cell at the police station, if he was well enough. And at the station he soon confessed and gave up his accomplices.

Strong boys of limited intellect, they freely, joyfully even, described the events of the night. Drunk after seeing their friend off to army duty, they recalled that the priest's house was nearby and decided to rob him. They'd heard that priests were wealthy. After breaking the window into the priest's house, they rummaged through his stuff in hope of finding something valuable; but, alas, there was nothing there. In the hallway, having decided on another room to ransack, one of them turned a door handle. Suddenly, there was a shot. With their partner wounded in his hand, they absconded. They managed to bandage him up a bit and headed to the hospital, afraid that the wound might get worse.

The investigation proceeded easily and swiftly. There was one thing, however, which confused these guys, and they eagerly looked to me for an explanation. Genuinely angry, they told me that since kindergarten days they'd been taught that priests were monsters and bloodsuckers, and that religion, to recall Lenin's lesson, was the opium of the masses. "Why, comrade detective, should we be put on trial because of some priest?"

It turned out that Father Nikodim, this "enemy of the people," was a very pleasant man; he had a lively and intelligent face. And he wasn't merely a priest, but was the rural dean, that is, the head priest of the entire district. He had an engineering degree. Before joining the clergy, he'd graduated from a mining institute and worked as an engineer in a mine. The mine collapsed and he was trapped there with other miners. Many of them perished, but he was miraculously saved. After the accident, he began to contemplate the meaning of life, which is what led him ultimately to a religious seminary.

I finished investigating Vengrenyuk and his friends' case by the deadline and forwarded everything we had to the court. I had long forgotten about it when Father Nikodim came unexpectedly to my office and asked for a little of my time

You're of the Jewish faith, right?"

"I'm a pureblooded Jew, Father," I answered.

"And I, as you know, am a Christian." He continued: "We are people of different faiths, but we share the same commandments. One of them is 'Thou shalt not kill!'—and I broke this commandment when I shot an innocent man who I could have killed."

Father Nikodim's anxiety was palpable. I tried to comfort him, insisting that he'd had no choice but to shoot in self-defense. He said he'd used the same reasoning when summoned by the leaders of the Church. But they paid no heed, arguing that a priest cannot shoot a fellow human being under any circumstances. If his actions were recorded in the court verdict, he told me, he would lose his position. Thus, a man's lawful behavior, prompted by the principle of self-defense, appeared to be in clear contradiction with the postulates of his religion. What should have been an honorable act—defending his home and family from criminals—had become the cause of even more distress.

We sat quietly for a while. I was confounded by this sad story. But there was no point getting worked up about the Church's stance or try to change its mind. What could be done? An extreme situation called for an extreme solution.

"Listen, Father," I began, "what if it wasn't you who fired the rifle, but your wife?"

The priest didn't quite understand where I was going with this and calmly explained that if it was his wife who'd pulled the trigger, there'd be no problem, since she obviously wasn't a priest. But it had been him; his wife didn't even know how to hold a rifle. I tried to impress upon him that no one needed to know whether she could handle the rifle or not. He figured out what I was suggesting, looked at me in disbelief, and reminded me that to lie was also a sin. "Out of the two evils, Father, we have to choose the lesser," I concluded.

Father Nikodim was now fully on board. Thus, a Jewish detective and an Orthodox priest joined in a secret scheme—

to knowingly provide false evidence in court in the name of a greater justice. And a few days later, the court decided that the defendant had been wounded by a shot fired by the priest's spouse. Father Nikodim kept his position and continued to serve as the rural dean.[8]

# 3. Meir and Khoma

These people have been gone for many years now. Khoma perished at the end of March 1944. Meir Katz died at the end of 1960s when he was tragically run over by a car. Meir lived in Krasyliv. Before the war it was a shtetl, whose old-timers claimed that Kasrilovka in Sholem Aleichem's stories was in fact their Krasyliv. Khoma lived in the village of Shchyborivka on the border with Krasyliv. Meir and Khoma were of the same age—about forty—but they were neither friends nor even good acquaintances; they simply knew each other as neighbors.

On the eve of the war, Meir worked as an accountant in a local store and Khoma worked in a kolkhoz. He was Jewish and Khoma was Ukrainian. I cannot provide the latter's last name, since I never learned what it was, and Meir never mentioned it; and it didn't occur to me to ask Meir and write it down. For him, Khoma was always just Khoma. The realization that I should have found out about his last name came much later, after Khoma and his family had left Krasyliv and I'd moved to a different city. At that stage, my attempts to find out Khoma's last name came to nothing. I'm recording here only what I learned from Meir's sorrowful story; my goal is to ensure that their names enter the annals of history and the reader's memory.

## 3. Meir and Khoma

In 1957, shortly after I was transferred to Krasyliv as a detective in the district attorney's office, I checked out an anonymous tip about abuses in the local store's procurement office. As Meir Katz, the manager of leather storage in the office, was one of our suspects, I called him in for questioning. A man of approximately fifty years of age stood in front of me, slightly shorter than average, and with a clearly Jewish face. He conducted himself in a calm manner, explaining, arguing, denying, and answering my questions, all without emotion. As soon as he left my office, the district attorney's secretary, the all-knowledgeable Larisa Semenovna, came up to me and said: "This man, by the way, was in Krasyliv during the Nazi occupation; he was in hiding."

Everything about the war was deeply personal to me. The Nazis murdered many of my family members—grandmothers, grandfather, aunts, and a lot of others. My father died in the battles for the liberation of Kyiv; I myself fought and was wounded at the front. That is why I asked the secretary to call in Meir again. He was soon back in my office. He didn't ask anything and waited patiently for my questions. He must have thought I needed to clarify something in the report. I apologized and asked him to tell me about himself, how he lived through and survived the war years in Krasyliv. He could have reacted in all sorts of ways to my request: politely decline because he was too busy or get angry and say I had no right to delve into a past he wanted to forget. But he did neither and agreed to tell his story.

Perhaps he sensed that my intentions were sincere. There was also another reason, possibly. The whole of Krasyliv had heard of him because in the immediate postwar years he'd been a witness in a several local trials of Nazi collaborators.

A good deal of time, however, had passed; not only were the trials many years ago, but the accused had been pardoned by the state and were alive and well.

Before I met with Katz, a number of antisemitic waves swept through the Soviet Union. First, there was the anticosmopolitan campaign, then there was the doctors' plot. The stench of antisemitism had become a permanent fixture in the country, and I experienced it as well. In this atmosphere, there was no interest in Katz and his story. This was why, I think, he wanted to tell me—a fellow Jew he believed would care—what he'd lived through. So we lit cigarettes and I listened to him without interrupting.

When the war broke out, Meir was not able to evacuate and stayed with his family in Krasyliv. The ghetto, where the Germans herded Jews from the nearby areas, was set up in the town of Starokonstantyniv, forty-five kilometers away from Krasyliv. I'm not writing anything about Katz's children, about how they perished. Meir didn't talk about them, and I didn't ask, seeing how painful it was for him to remember the horror. All I know is that by the time he met Khoma in the ghetto, Meir's children were already dead.

One sunny summer Sunday in 1941, an encounter took place which turned out to be fateful for both of them. Khoma went to a market in Starokonstantyniv, where, passing ghetto's fence, he spotted Meir. They had a brief conversation; it was dangerous to stick around too long. Khoma proposed that Meir escape to Khoma's place in Shchyborivka.

One night, Katz and his wife dug under the fence and ran. It took them two days to reach Khoma's house. They would walk during the night and hide in the forest and the ravines during the day. Khoma was waiting for them. He'd dug a large pit in his barn and put a makeshift bed and a little table there; and when the escapees arrived their shelter was ready.

Khoma gathered his family—his wife and children—and told them: "The Germans want to kill these people because they're Jews. That's why they are here. We need to make sure that no one is killed. From this day forward we have to do everything the Germans and their collaborators demand. I forbid you from bringing anything into the house; we can't give them any reason to search here."

And so began this simple man's great mission to save two Jewish lives. It lasted for more than two and a half years. Throughout the long days and nights, Meir and his wife sat in the pit with the cattle, getting out only a few times when it was dark. For two and a half years Khoma's family constantly risked their lives. Every night, Khoma would descend into the pit to bring Meir and his wife some food and tell them what was happening in Krasyliv. He told them that Meir's former boss, Gavrilyuk, the store manager, had been installed as the new mayor of Krasyliv by the Germans. At Meir's request, Khoma got hold of a gun, which he then gave to the escapee.

In the spring of 1942, Khoma told Meir that three women who were trying to cross over to the Romanian side were hiding in the forest not far from them. Mayor Gavrilyuk had now moved out of his apartment and into a mansion the Germans designated for him. One evening, a man walked unannounced into Gavrilyuk's mansion office. He was dirty, had long hair, and smelt of dirt and manure. It was Meir Katz, of course. Unsurprisingly, Gavrilyuk did not recognize him immediately, but when he did, he wasn't shocked.

"It's good you came here by choice, Meir," he said. "We would have found you in any case. You've done the right thing; it's time to meet your destiny."

"No," Meir replied, "that's not why I came. I need passports for three women. Give them to me."

The mayor was stunned, but overcoming his initial shock he started to laugh. "You dirty miserable Jew," he finally uttered through his laughter. "How dare you say this to me; you must have lost your mind."

"I need three passports," Katz repeated. "Give them to me. One day these passports and I will serve you well."

The mayor laughed again and said: "Before the fat one gets thin, the thin one will croak."

As they were speaking, Gavrilyuk's wife, who knew Meir well, entered the office. She was astonished by his appearance. Meir explained to her why he was there. She kneeled before her husband and begged him to get the passports, but Gavrilyuk chased her away. Sitting behind his desk, he removed a gun from the drawer and pointed it at Meir, only to discover that his former employee already had a gun on him. "Put the gun away," Katz said. "Why risk a shootout with me? You're satisfied with your life and value it. I have a death sentence hanging over me; my life is worth nothing. Put it away." The mayor did as he was told, and Katz left.

Why Gavrilyuk decided not to have his people pursue Katz, which, of course, he could have done, I don't know. Katz did not say anything about this; I only listened, asking him nothing. The answer is in the material in the criminal case against Gavrilyuk, perhaps. What is certain is that while hiding from death in the barn, Meir took a risk and made a desperate attempt to save three fellow Jews he did not know.

The war's ended and the Nazis were driven away. Gavrilyuk tried to flee with them, but he was caught and brought back to Krasyliv, where he was put on trial. Meir acted as a witness. During the investigation, a meeting was arranged between them to gather the details of their conversation in the mansion. In the detective's office, Meir said to Gavrilyuk: "See, you got thin, but I didn't croak."

At the beginning of March 1944, Krasyliv was liberated from the German occupiers. Meir and his wife emerged from their shelter into the light of day, but they were not destined to sit at the festive table with Khoma and raise glasses to one another. Khoma had volunteered to lead the troops tracking down the retreating Germans. He got inside the tank next to the soldiers and was killed in battle, an unarmed warrior who'd already performed a great act of bravery.

Until his last day, Meir was like a father to Khoma's children; they called him Pops in Ukrainian. The lives of the Jew Meir and the Ukrainian Khoma were entwined. May their memories be a blessing.

\*\*\*

As I finished writing this piece, I received a letter from Vinnytsya. My sister, Nella Goldis, who lived there and would soon join us in America, unearthed at my request not just Khoma's last name, but that his daughter still lived in her native village, Shchyborivka. Now I knew that Khoma was Khoma Vasylevich Matsyuk and that his daughter was Solomiya Khomivna Ukrainets. I could have edited my story in light of this new information, but I decided not to change anything. Let Khoma stay as he always was for Meir as he was for me all these years—simply Khoma.[9]

# 4. Guilty without Guilt

The Khmelnytskyi region was bursting with excitement caused by the arrival of the new regional boss. This was Oleksiy Vatchenko, appointed as the first secretary of the region's party committee (later he will become Speaker of Ukraine's supreme council). Sensational stories traveled rapidly about who he was and what he might do. Since hardly anyone knew what Vatchenko looked like, he could easily pay incognito visits to factories, organizations, stores, markets, and cultural venues; in other words, he could ascertain their faults and ruthlessly punish the culprits. Soon after his arrival, new industrial, commercial, and cultural sites rapidly sprung up around the region. Gossip and hearsay surrounded him during his first days as first secretary, making it impossible to separate fact and fiction. There was no doubt, however, that an energetic and tough-minded man was the new sheriff in town.

Krasyliv's party committee held a plenary devoted to fighting crime in the area. A number of law enforcement representatives were invited, including me as a detective in the district attorney's office. Vatchenko was naturally in attendance too. I looked forward to seeing and listening to him up close and personal.

Adhering to the standard formalities, the plenum's agenda was moving in a predictably slow manner. Suddenly, however,

## 4. Guilty without Guilt

someone in the audience handed a note to the chairman. He perused it and immediately passed it along to Vatchenko. He got up, his enormous stomach hanging over the table and read it out loud. The note stated that while the plenary was discussing the issues of fighting crime, there was a criminal sitting among its participants: Grigory Golder, the head of the Road to Communism kolkhoz. I knew Golder, as I knew every other kolkhoz head in the district through my detective work. He and I were on good, that is, professional terms and never discussed any Jewish topics; but I held him in high regard because he was one of the handful of Jews in charge of a kolkhoz in the entire Ukraine. His facial features were also typically or even stereotypically Jewish.

"Is Golder here?" Vatchenko inquired. Golder stood up, ready to answer the party boss's questions in front of the entire audience. "Is what the note says true?" Vatchenko asked.

"No, not true: I never embezzled any kolkhoz funds," Golder responded.

"But you did take ten thousand rubles from the kolkhoz cashbox, yes?"

"Yes, I did."

"Did you return the money to the kolkhoz or do you still have it?" Vatchenko was relentless.

"No, I did not return the money and I do not have it . . . ," Golder said.

"Are you able to present any documents in your defense?"

"No, I cannot. I don't have any documents, but I can explain, how I spent the money . . ."

"You will have to explain that somewhere else!" Vatchenko shouted.

Vatchenko ordered the judge, the chief attorney, and the police chief, all of whom were in the audience, to stand up. Looking at them as if they were a law enforcement trinity, he demanded that they immediately decide the punishment for the thieving Golder. Vatchenko told those in the presidium to revoke Golder's party membership right there and then. This was voted on and the result was unanimous. Golder was asked to turn in his party membership card and leave the plenary. He placed his party card on the table in front of the committee and left the hall.

When the door shut behind Golder, Vatchenko got up again and yelled: "Do not be surprised, comrades . . . This is in their blood; they're used to profiting on the people's backs. No mercy for them, we've got to hit them on their bonces—their bonces!" He finished and banged his huge fist on the table.

Apart from me, there were one or two other Jews in the audience. Looking back on this episode, I wish all of the Jews had stood and, rejecting this hateful travesty, followed Golder out of the door. Yet, we did not stir and sat with our faces turning crimson, not daring to look at anyone, as if, indeed, some sort of diseased blood flowed through our veins. I had already witnessed antisemitism in various manifestations and bore its scars on my own skin; but I was amazed by what I heard come out of the regional leader's mouth. The first secretary of the region's party committee, a politician of high rank, was spewing primitive and shameless hatred. I had gone to the plenary hoping to see an interesting person I'd heard so much about. Instead, I left bitter, hurt, and disillusioned.

Anxious to please his master, the region's chief attorney ordered an immediate criminal investigation into Golder and stated that he wanted the matter concluded as speedily as possible. Golder would be arrested within days. Ironically, the Jew Goldis was entrusted with hitting the Jew Golder on the bonce.

I summoned Golder to my office. He had been stripped of his position in charge of his kolkhoz. As I knew from experience, all sorts of people were heads of kolkhozes—competent, incompetent, or simply dishonest. Never, however, had I met one who was a complete half-wit, so I was sure that Golder had thought long and hard about his situation and come up with a good explanation in his defense. To my utter astonishment, he answered my question about what he had done with the ten thousand rubles with a simple answer: "I spent it on booze."

"You must be joking," I blurted out, "now is not the time for jokes."

Golder then proceeded to tell a straightforward and banal story.

The kolkhoz had a problem. It didn't have enough space for its cattle, so it was necessary to decide between slaughtering the animals or trying to find, by any means possible, construction materials for building a cowshed and a pigsty. He went with the second option. Golder traveled to the Ivano-Frankivsk region, where he found a bunch of "entrepreneurs" associated with the forest department; he fed them and drank with them for a week, spending five thousand rubles in the process, while they got him the wood he wanted. Afterwards, he traveled to Dnipropetrovsk, Vatchenko's home region, and spent another five thousand rubles in the same way and on iron roofing. Then he took all this material back to his kolkhoz.

Once I'd written down his testimony, Golder asked me to add documents to the case file showing that the cowshed and pigsty had been built. He also asked to photograph the constructions and get an invoice from the district executive committee specifying the materials used.

I followed Golder's requests to the letter. The result was twofold: there was no official documentation from the committee, but there were photos of the two good-looking, newly built farmhouses. The most interesting detail was that the officials who voted unanimously to revoke his party membership and throw him to the courts knew about the cowshed and pigsty. It took me a while to gather all the evidence, as the chief attorney was breathing down my neck, urging me to make an arrest. Another challenge was finding the people Golder paid for getting the construction materials. A detective was sent to assist me, and we got ready to go to Ivano-Frankivsk and Dnipropetrovsk. Much remained to be done, but I was convinced that Golder didn't embezzle any money. He had, indeed, bypassed the law, given kolkhoz funds to some crooks, but he never pocketed any of the money himself.

I had to present a report about it to my bosses. The denunciation of Golder—the accusation that he had criminal Jewish blood and should be hit over the head—made the task ahead of me very difficult. But a helping hand came from the most unexpected place. The first secretary of the district's party committee called me up and invited me to discuss Golder's case with him. I set out the case at a meeting with him and a representative of the region's party committee. They asked me whether other heads of kolkhozes obtained construction materials in a similar fashion. I answered that I didn't have any data or documentary proof to that effect, but that if they wanted personal opinion, I was sure that others were doing exactly the same. They simply had no choice.

The party bureaucrats pondered the matter in silence and then told me that there was a general feeling that the proceedings against Golder should be stopped. I was shocked. All the recent events rushed through my head: Golder's excommunication from the party, his ejection from the meeting hall, his dismissal from his job . . . I managed to keep my emotions in check and told them that since the proceedings were initiated by direct order of the chief attorney, they could only be stopped by a similar order. I also reminded them about who had instigated this whole business and left the office.

Soon after, the chief attorney told Vatchenko about Golder's case. Vatchenko not only agreed to halt the investigation, but issued a directive to reinstate his party membership and reappoint him as the head of the kolkhoz. I don't know what guided his thinking. Did he feel a pang of conscience about his shameful antisemitic display? I don't know, but hope he did.

I stopped the criminal proceedings against Golder. Krasyliv's district party committee quietly, but unanimously, reinstated his party membership and gave him back—again hush-hush, without witnesses—his card. Grigory Golder declined the invitation to be reinstated as the leader of his kolkhoz.[10]

# 5. On the Shores of the River Bug

Two criminal cases—involving different events, people, and circumstances—have merged in my memory to form a single narrative. Both of them took place in the Vinnytsya region, both were investigated by me in the early 1960s, and both concerned the deaths of two young men. Misha Prokhorov and Zhenya Myasnikov had just turned nineteen when they were carried away by the waters of the River Bug their lives cut short. These incidents led to protracted investigations by various detectives who arrived invariably at the same conclusion: the boys had drowned and no one was to blame.

Yet it wasn't the similarities of these deaths that made me conflate these cases in my mind; it was the boys' mothers. They were very unlike each other in appearance. Misha's mother, Anna Ivanovna, was short, thin, and had dark hair. Zhenya's mother, Nathalya Mikhailovna, was tall and stout, and had her grey hair in a bun at the back of the neck. These women also came from different social backgrounds. Prokhorova was a poorly educated village woman who worked in a kolkhoz; Myasnikova lived in Vinnytsya, a regional center, and was a teacher. Their demeanor couldn't be more different: Prokhorova was rough and twitchy, while Myasnikova was soft and delicate in her manners. They were single mothers and had no other children beside their sons, and this fact intensified their feelings of motherly love and compassion.

When their sons died, on a clear blue day, they didn't retreat into their grief. Instead, they curled themselves up into tight balls, like hedgehogs, and tried to prove, tirelessly, persistently, and in the face of bureaucratic indifference, that their boys were victims of brutal crimes rather than carelessness. Thanks to their efforts, the deaths of Prokhorov and Myasnikov became of interest to people at the highest levels of Ukrainian and federal Soviet law enforcement.

### *In the Village of Uladivka*

In 1961, Ivan Protsyuk's gang, responsible for years of terror in the Krasyliv district, was finally neutralized. I was praised by the chief attorney for this success, and my career benefited significantly. He asked me if I wanted to transfer to his office in Khmelnytskyi, where I would become a senior detective. This was a flattering offer. It would mean promotion to a higher rank and a move from a godforsaken provincial town to the region's capital. I agreed without giving the idea a second thought.

Soon after taking up my new position, Soviet Ukraine's attorney general's office appointed me as supervisor of the Prokhorov case. Excited and impatient to begin, I read the two folders of material about the matter; it was the first time in my career that I had worked at the direct behest of the republic's attorney general. The volumes consisted of the usual—interrogation minutes, forensic examinations, and other documents—but also Prokhorov's mother's letters of complaint and responses to them. Earlier the case was terminated five times due to the lack of any evidence pointing to a crime:

Prokhorov's death was still considered an accident. However, the attorney general's office restarted the investigation five times.

I was baffled by the two folders. What a boringly typical story! In 1960, one summer evening, Mikhail Prokhorov, a resident of the village of Uladivka in the Vinnytsya region, nineteen years of age, did not return home. Three days later, his body was discovered in the Bug River, seven kilometers away from his place of residence.

According to the forensic expert, drowning was the cause of death; no signs of injury were found on Prokhorov's body, except for a small hematoma on the back of his head, which could have resulted from hitting a sharp object when he fell to the water. "There was no causal relationship between this injury and Prokhorov's death," the forensic expert stated. That was basically that. My God, so many accidents like that happened in every district, especially during the summer time, especially involving young people. Rivers do not forgive sloppiness or lack of caution; they mercilessly swallow human beings.

In every ruling canceling the case, it was asserted that Prokhorov fell while walking at night on an old bridge without any rails; he lost balance, plummeted into the river from a height of five hundred meters, and drowned. It was deemed that no criminal proceedings were necessary. But now there was a year and a half's material regarding Prokhorov—two thick folders—and the attorney general was involved. What was going on? The boy's mother was behind it all. She claimed that her son was killed. Law enforcement should have expected this view, of course; relatives tend to come to this conclusion when a loved one dies in unusual circumstances and without anyone around, that is, neither at home nor in hospital. Prokhorova was typical in this respect. However, she also named the person she thought was the murderer—her neighbor, Vasily Yaremchuk, who lived just across the street from her house.

The day after her son's disappearance, a neighbor told Prokhorova that he had heard a noise in Yaremchuk's front yard at around midnight the previous night; it had sounded like someone being hit or falling over. When we interviewed him, however, the neighbor claimed that he'd heard this commotion much earlier and not on the day of Prokhorov's disappearance. He'd mixed up the days. He wouldn't budge from his statement; meanwhile, the victim's mother insisted that he'd changed his testimony under pressure from Yaremchuk and his wife, a very important person in the village. They'd threatened or bribed the witness.

The Yaremchuks' complaints were also in the folder. These seemingly honest, hardworking people wanted to be shielded from Prokhorova's baseless accusations. However, she kept writing to the authorities, filling pages torn from lined school notebooks and receiving in response the same explanation that there was no evidence that her son had been murdered by Yaremchuk or anyone else. On the contrary, everything clearly pointed to the fact that her son had fallen from a rickety old bridge at night and drowned in the river. It's true that there was no witness, but it's impossible to see everyone who falls into the river, right?

Prokhorova was unpersuaded. She was convinced that no one wanted to find out the truth, that they were just going through the motions. The residents of Uladivka and the nearby villages collected money for her to travel to Kyiv and then Moscow, where she waited patiently for days to be seen by the most important people in Ukrainian and Soviet enforcement. And so the death of an unknown young man drew the attention of the central party as well as the Ukrainian and federal authorities.

Thanks to Prokhorova's efforts, the status of the case changed dramatically. Its merits were reviewed and it became of the utmost importance to reach the correct verdict. Reading through the two folders, the regional attorney's office found multiple problems with the investigation; the case was reopening and I was finally appointed. I finished studying the files, feeling lost and distraught again. What was I, yet another detective, supposed to do? Revisit everything that had been decided on many times before? I didn't want to do that, but I had no idea what else to do.

The large village of Uladivka, where I arrived at the beginning of January 1962, sprawled along the Bug River. There were two factories in it—a sugar plant and a distillery—and a railway station. On the day of my arrival, I met with Anna Prokhorova. Our meeting was brief. She asked me if I'd come to conduct a real investigation or just hang around like the detectives and then leave. It was an offensive question and I could have reacted to it accordingly, but, looking into her dark eyes, filled with suffering, terror, and suspense, I realized that I shouldn't stoop to her level. I answered that I was going to find out what really happened and would do my best.

A routine for the investigation was established. I called people in for questioning, examined the bridge from which Prokhorov allegedly fell, examined the section of the village where the Prokhorovs, Yaremchuks, and their neighbors lived. Thus, a week went by during which I analyzed everything

I saw and heard, trying to work out the truth. By the end of the week, I had arrived at certain conclusions.

In Prokhorov's case, there were two main theories: the first was that he fell from the bridge and drowned; the second was that he was killed by Yaremchuk. It was obvious that the first version was factual, supported by the discovery of Prokhorov's body, while the second was completely baseless. Only the victim's mother insisted on its veracity. The investigation settled on the first version and proceeded with it for a year and a half like a well-oiled machine. It was as though Prokhorov's case was placed in the river and it swam along until it stopped at the spot by the bridge where the poor boy's body was found, his clothes snagged on a rock.

I was tempted to once more follow course trodden by the former detectives, but instead chose another path and decided to go against the current. Why did I make such a sharp turn? During my first week in the village, I received no new material or testimonial evidence about the causes of Prokhorov's demise. Even before I arrived in Uladivka, I realized that I wouldn't be able to find anything, considering how much time had elapsed since the incident. My conclusions came about as a result of purely subjective reasoning and intuition.

According to the forensic experts, Prokhorov died between midnight and two o'clock in the morning. They couldn't determine with any precision why he happened to be on the bridge at such a late hour, though, so far from home. There was a suggestion that he was there for a date with a girl, but no such girl was found. I was alarmed by the fact that during all this time no information supported the idea that amorous adventures brought Prokhorov to the fateful bridge. When this question started to trouble me, Prokhorova's mother told me that any talk about a rendezvous with a girl was nonsense; he hadn't yet developed an interest in women. I saw that Prokhorova was a sincere person and believed her, thinking to myself: "What if there's no proof of Prokhorov's walk on the bridge because he never was on the bridge?" As ancient wisdom says, it's very difficult to look for a black cat in a dark room, especially if there's no cat there.

One of the people I called in for questioning during my first week in Uladivka was the neighbor who claimed to have heard a noise in Yaremchuk's front yard at night. The previous detectives had already questioned him many times, so it wasn't surprising that it was his testimony that had given Prokhorov good reason to think that Yaremchuk was the killer.

I do not recall this man's last name. Even before I started questioning him, he quickly began to offer his well-polished testimony. He insisted that he saw Yaremchuk in his front yard one night and heard noises—but that it had been before the time of Prokhorov's disappearance. He was like a student who had memorized his lesson and was reciting it, understanding nothing about the content. I sensed that he was lying. This again was a purely subjective feeling, but once it took hold of me, it significantly affected my subsequent decisions. It was obvious that someone needed this person to lie, that someone needed the noise in Yaremchuk's front yard to be way earlier than the time of Prokhorov's disappearance. Who could it be? The Yaremchuks, of course.

Prokhorova drew my attention to the fact that whenever Yaremchuk was called in for questioning, his wife, Sofia, accompanied him. And the same thing happened when I summoned him. There didn't seem to be anything peculiar about the wife joining her husband, but I started to think that she was worried that her simpleminded Vasily might blurt something out, and that she wanted to be there to make sure he didn't.

Such were my thoughts—so I put aside the idea that Prokhorov fell from the bridge and took Yaremchuk's involvement in the death of his young neighbor seriously. But how could this theory be verified? What proof of Yaremchuk's guilt or innocence could I find a year and a half after the event? It occurred to me that I could ask him directly whether he was guilty or not. I just had to do it without the presence of his better half. He had to be alone with his conscience.

Thus, a decision was made to arrest Yaremchuk. In order for this to happen one main obstacle needed to be overcome, namely Mrs. Yaremchuk. Intelligent, willful, beautiful, and with good managerial skills, she was a rising local politician and could soon become a deputy in the Ukrainian soviet. But suddenly, her glorious trajectory was obstructed by Anna Prokhorova who accused Yaremchuk of committing the most heinous of crimes. It was clear that the smart and energetic Sofia would do everything in her power to divert the threatening cloud that hung over her and her husband's heads. Additionally, she had strong protectors among important local party bureaucrats. The district attorney warned me in advance, without mincing his words, that it would be wise not to get involved with this dame; there'd be hell to pay.

However, I made two major decisions: first, I chose to conduct the investigation in a way that would pacify Sofia; second, I resolved to arrest Yaremchuk in Vinnytsya rather than in his native village or nearby. I managed to create the impression that I was following in the footsteps of my predecessors regarding Prokhorov's fall from the bridge; I pretended that I was fed up with the case and wanted to be done with it as soon as possible; I even started a rumor that a deadline was coming up that I had to leave shortly.

So I announced that I was going to Vinnytsya in order to write a report for the attorney general in Kyiv. I also left a list of witnesses, which included Yaremchuk, with the head of the village council, informing him that I had a few outstanding questions for them and would need to continue my questioning in Vinnytsya. I was sure that this information would be passed on to Sofia Yaremchuk who, I suspected, would try to prevent her husband's detention. Instead of using a local policeman, I asked for an officer to be sent from Vinnytsya. Luckily for me they sent Captain Konstantin Mashchenko from the criminal investigation squad. Mashchenko was a policeman with absolute integrity; he resembled in both his appearance and demeanor the Detective Captain Gleb Zheglov, played by the legendary Vladimir Vysotsky in the cult TV series *The Meeting Place Cannot Be Changed*.[11] Mashchenko agreed with my approach and supported Yaremchuk's arrest.

On the appointed day, Mashchenko and I waited for Yaremchuk at the Vinnytsya police headquarters, worried that the cunning Sophia had discovered my plan and that he wouldn't show up. He did arrive, however, and was accompanied, of course, by his wife. I invited him into my office and announced that he would be held in custody and was suspected of Prokhorov's murder. Then I informed Sophia Yaremchuk of her husband's situation.

Within two hours, I was notified that I should immediately call the region's chief attorney in Khmelnytskyi; it was clear that Sofia Yaremchuk was on the march. She rushed to the attorney general's office and complained that some detective from Khmelnytskyi had arrested an innocent man and needed to be stopped. The attorney general ordered the chief attorney in Khmelnytskyi to immediately clarify the matter. During our phone conversation, the latter ordered me to release Yaremchuk. I refused and told him I'd report to him in Khmelnytskyi.

The chief attorney of the Khmelnytskyi region was Nikolai Lyashenko, a young, energetic, and knowledgeable attorney who would serve in this important position for the next twenty years.[12] In 1962, he was only forty-one years old. A veteran of the Battle of Stalingrad, where he lost an arm, he'd formerly worked in Donbass, one of the most crime-ridden regions in postwar Ukraine. When we met, his fury was palpable, but I looked past it and began to explain what I'd learned about the Prokhorov affair since my arrival in Uladivka. My account was very emotional and well conveyed my anxieties and concerns. I admitted that I had no solid grounds for arresting Yaremchuk, but felt that it was necessary in order to at least convey to the boy's poor mother that we had done everything in our power to find out what had happened to her son.

Lyashneko signed the warrant for Yaremchuk's arrest, and the next day, when he was informed of the warrant, he asked to be interrogated again. He was brought into my office, where he finally recounted the sad story of Mikhail Prokhorov's murder.

The Yaremchuks kept rabbits in their backyard, which were often stolen. Determined to catch the thief, Yaremchuk stumbled one night upon Misha Prokhorov trying to get a rabbit out of its cage. Yaremchuk picked up a wooden pole from the ground, snuck up on him, and struck the boy, from behind, on the head. Prokhorov fell. Yaremchuk hadn't intended to kill the thief. Seeing what he'd done, he put the body in a large sack, took it to the river three to four hundred meters away, and threw it in the water. He then burned the pole and the sack.

We asked Yaremchuk to go with us to the site of the incident. He refused, telling us that he'd be too ashamed to look people in the eye. We proposed doing it at night, and thus, he reenacted events in the slumbering village under the cover of darkness.

I returned to Uladivka to finish what I'd set out to do—get hold of an expert to determine whether Prokhorov's body could have been carried by the river from where Yaremchuk threw it in the water. He would need to gather data about the river. The kolkhoz provided me with a team of workers, who made markings in the river every four hundred meters, seven kilometers in total, while the specialist checked the depth of the river. I also received data from the hydraulic station about the temperature of the river on the day of Prokhorov's disappearance, as well as the speed of the current. The expert concluded that the boy's body could have been carried by the river within forty-eight hours.

Yaremchuk was sure that he'd killed Prokhorov and thrown a dead body in the river. Yet, according to the expert, the boy had drowned: he was still alive in the water. The contradiction between Yaremchuk's testimony and the claim of the expert could only be resolved through a forensic examination of the body; thus, it had to be exhumed. I felt that it had to be carried by Kyiv's best forensic expert—so I put in a request during my subsequent visit there and it was approved.

I got back to Uladivka and met the expert at the train station late at night. I have to admit I was somewhat surprised when, instead of a male specialist, a young and attractive woman stepped out onto the platform. Her name was Evgeniya Ivanovna. Exhumation is a very difficult procedure, and it is emotional and painful for everyone involved. I've seen many exhumations in my life and have heard many stories about them—they're worthy of a separate chapter.

As I was speaking with the kolkhoz head about forming a team to open up Prokhorov's grave, the boy's mother walked in. She already knew what we were discussing and asked whether the exhumation could be avoided. I answered in the negative. She found out the time when the coffin would be lifted out and said that no one but her would remove her son from his resting place.

The next day, Prokhorov's petrified mother stood by the coffin on the edge of the open grave; I don't know how she was able to bear it, or who assisted her. For the first time in my career, I saw the rock-like resolve of a desperate mother. The experts concluded that the blow to the back of the head caused the boy to lose consciousness. Yaremchuk had interpreted this as death. The boy might have survived had he not been thrown in the river.

The investigation was over. I put together an indictment, which was approved by the region's chief prosecutor, and forwarded it to the court. Yaremchuk received a ten-year prison sentence for the manslaughter of Prokhorov. I was then summoned to the attorney general's office in Kyiv, who offered his gratitude. He wrote in praise of my work and rewarded me financially. I returned to Khmelnytskyi, flying high on the wings of success.

Soon thereafter my boss called me in. He told me that he had received a directive from the regional party committee to remove me from the regional attorney's office because I was a Jew; he also swore me to secrecy. The higher-ups couldn't care less about my successes and professional abilities. They were administering their policy of frenzied antisemitism, incomprehensible even to such faithful servants of the regime as the region's chief attorney.

The party bosses asked my boss to find a suitable reason for sending me back to the district. He did not do this, told me everything, and offered to send me to a district of my choice. My pick was the ancient city of Kamyanets-Podilskyi.[13]

## *A Brief Epilogue*

In 1965, once more in Uladivka, two boys disappeared. The whole village searched for them for a long time, with military units assisting; but it was all in vain. Inevitably, rumors started to spread about murder. A criminal case was opened up, but nothing was found. Then the villagers remembered Prokhorov's case and the detective with a mind of his own.

A delegation from Uladivka was sent to the attorney general's office in Kyiv; the people demanded, on behalf of the whole village, that I look into the boys' disappearance, and I received a directive from the attorney general to assist the attorney's office of the Vinnytsya region. Thus, unexpectedly, I ended up in Uladivka again. On the day after my arrival, I went to see Anna Prokhorova. We met in her front yard; she was glad and excited to see me, and so was I.

## *Unfulfilled Retribution*

At the behest of the attorney general of Soviet Ukraine, I was tasked with leading a criminal investigation into the death of one Myasnikov in the city of Vinnytsya. This was the summer of 1963, a little more than a year after I'd solved the Prokhorov case in Uladivka. Chief Attorney Lyashenko was visibly displeased with my appointment to the case, but prohibited from challenging the decisions, he had no choice but to let me go to Vinnytsya.

I received the case materials from the regional attorney's office in Vinnytsya and buried myself in the four-year-old evidence. One bright day in September in 1959, around four o'clock in the afternoon, Evgeny Myasnikov, a student at the city's medical institute, put on a new white shirt and headed out to meet his girlfriend. She lived in a private house on the outskirts of the city, in an affluent neighborhood by the Bug River. Many of the houses were protected by metal fences and had either a car or a motorcycle parked in the front yard. I do not recall any names of the people who lived on the adjacent street and who were directly related to the investigation. Here I will simply refer to them as "owners," a term often used in court proceedings. Not far from the student's girlfriend's house, a Volga (the Soviet Cadillac) was parked. Its doors were open. Myasnikov got in, sat at the wheel, and honked a few times. He then released the hand brake—the car was parked on a slope—and the automobile started to roll down the hill. After about two hundred meters, it stopped on the road and Myasnikov got out.

Suddenly, he saw a group of people brandishing rifles, shovels, and clubs, running toward him, yelling. When Evgeny had gotten into the car, the owner's ten-year-old son had spotted him and rushed off to tell his dad that someone was stealing the car. The owner had grabbed his rifle and run outside, calling to his neighbors for assistance. In total, six people had joined him.

Seeing the angry group approaching, Myasnikov took off in the only possible direction—toward the river right behind him. He stepped into the water and hid in the reeds. He did not return home, and two days later was discovered dead in the river. According to the forensic expert, his death was from drowning; there were no signs of injuries found on the body. And that was that. Again, we had the River Bug and the death of a young man.

The case materials contained two documents of interest: the first was Myasnikov's mother's demand that those culpable for her son's death be criminally charged; the second was a request from the car owner to be shielded from the mother's unfounded accusations. The file also contained a directive to close the case and a later one to reopen it.

The number of people brought in for questioning grew and grew because they all lived on the same street as the car owner who pursued Myasnikov. Some of them heard a scream, others witnessed the chase. None of these new witnesses added anything to the exhaustive and apparently honest accounts already given by the six neighbors who ran after the boy. It was true, they admitted, that they followed the student and were armed with whatever they could find. After all, it looked like Myasnikov was trying to steal the car in broad daylight. And yes, they eventually realized that he wasn't a thief and that, in fact, he was visiting one of their neighbor's daughters, honking simply to call the girl and impress her. But that was later. First, they tried to catch him so they could hand him over to the police. They saw him hiding in the reeds and told him to give himself up. One of them drove around the reeds, calling on Myasnikov, but he neither responded nor came out. After they waited for twenty or thirty minutes, the men went back to their homes and forgot about the whole business.

Everything seemed clear, then: we knew when and why he ran toward the river, who chased him there, and where he entered the water. There was no evidence of any violence; there were no signs of injury on his body—not even a scratch. What was I supposed to investigate? Remembering Uladivka, though, I did not rush to any conclusions. Instead, I reexamined the site of the incident—the street of private houses, the road to the river, the boats tied to the shore, and the thickets of reeds. At the time, the Bug was a wide and navigable river. I would visit the site many times during the investigation, watch the water gently gliding by, and contemplate what to do next.

A few days after arriving from Vinnytsya, I met Nathalia Mikhailovna, Zhenya's mother. She believed that her son hadn't drowned, but that he had died at the hands of the angry car owner and his neighbors. She tried to support her theory by telling me that Zhenya was physically strong, swam like a pro, and even worked as a lifeguard at the city's pool during the summer. This claim, however, had been dismissed by previous detectives because of the absence of marks on the body. The evidence was irrefutable. Myasnikov had walked into the river on his own volition and could easily return to the shore within half an hour. The forensic expert and the witness statements all agreed on this.

I questioned everyone again. They repeated what they'd said previously, and answered my questions readily. They even asked me a question: What did I, a law enforcement officer, think of their actions? Had they been right to protect their property and try to apprehend someone they thought was a thief? They were in the right; I could find no legal fault in their actions. But I didn't say this to them directly because of the haunting words of the dead boy's mother: "Even if these people thought he was a criminal, it was inhuman to hound a him into the river and trap him there like an animal. There is no defense for that."

These heartrending words helped to divert me from the standard path of my colleagues; they forced the detective in me to dig deeper and look harder for the truth. Thus, I added Myasnikov's swimming certificate and a statement from the pool about his work there to the file. But if it was pointless questioning the people who lived on the street adjacent to the river or nearby, how should I proceed?

The river was wide. It was impossible to see anything on the opposite bank—and vice versa. However, ships sailed on the river with crews which may have seen or heard something. Thus, I decided to look for completely new witnesses. The chances of finding them were slim, considering the four years that had elapsed since the incident, but, as a detective, I had to do everything I could to expose the truth. I asked the river's shipping authority about the day in question and was informed that on September 27, 1959, a ship had passed through the area I was interested in.

It was a sightseeing ship carrying a group of children from an orphanage in a Vinnytsya suburb. It didn't quite match the timeframe I was after—between 4:00 p.m. and 5:00 p.m—but between 7:00 p.m. and 8:00 p.m. This gave me pause, but not enough to stop me. I called the orphanage and received some astounding information. They did not just confirm the fact that the children had been on a sightseeing excursion on the evening of September 27, 1959, but also provided me with a list of names and their current addresses. There were fifteen or sixteen boys and girls of twelve to fourteen years of age.

Now they were adults living all over Ukraine and beyond. Inspired by my discovery, I contacted the attorney offices near the addresses I had and instructed them to question the former passengers and report back to me.

Though I expected nothing significant, I received twelve reports, five or six of which turned out to be crucial for Myasnikov's case. The passengers recalled seeing, from the ship's deck, a few men rooting around at the edge of the river. They were talking loudly and shouting at someone in the reeds. It was getting dark and the men were pointing flashlights at a certain area while one of them drove around it in a boat. Then the new witnesses saw a man wearing a white shirt leave the reeds and start swimming toward the middle of the river. At the time they hadn't thought it was anything important, but there was no doubt that they'd seen Myasnikov—and just before his death, that is, when he'd been trying to escape his pursuers.

My strategy was coming together. The time discrepancy was a problem, but it was clear that the witnesses were giving the correct time. Their accounts were dispassionate; they knew neither Myasnikov nor the men. It was also significant that they were questioned separately, in different places, and by different detectives. And the time they gave for what they saw matched the ship's schedule.

All of this meant that Myasnikov hadn't been ambushed in the reeds for twenty or thirty minutes, as the original witnesses insisted, but for about three hours. That's hours in cold water, in wet clothes, and very frightened. Everything finally made sense. The boy's mother had said: "it was inhuman to hound him into the river and trap him there like an animal." It was now clear why a fit young man and an excellent swimmer had drowned. Indeed, like a hunted little animal, he was psychologically and physically exhausted.

The case took a drastic new turn. I was sure that a crime had been committed. But a decision had to be made about the criminal responsibility of the culprits, namely, what type of crime they had committed and what article of the criminal code addressed it. This was a deeply complex matter, considering the unusual nature of the case, but I was in no doubt that the people who'd chased Myasnikov had to stand trial and answer for his death.

I needed to establish a direct link between the actions of Myasnikov's pursuers and his drowning. My detective's guesswork would no longer suffice—I needed the help of experts. And because the case was so unusual, and was being overseen by the government and the attorney general of the USSR, I wanted to get someone from the main forensic division in the country.

I requested approval from the attorney general's office and then sent Myasnikov's case to the main forensic division. I asked the experts if they could find a causal connection between the pursuers' actions and the student's death; and added that I wanted them to do so without examining the corpse. I thought it was unnecessary. I was told that the examination could certainly go ahead, but that they would only do it if I also provided some bones from the deceased's skull and extremities. In a repetition of the Prokhorov case a year earlier, I once more found myself having to do most awful thing: exhume a corpse.

I issued the necessary order and left for Vinnytsya with the head of the regional forensic division, Fillip Vyskrebtsov. This was the first of multiple future visits to the Vinnytsya city cemetery. Indeed, my mother would find her eternal rest there eight years later.

Prior to the start of the exhumation, I told Nathalia Myasnikova why it had to be done. I remembered the stoicism with which Mikhail Prokhorov's mother has dealt with the opening of her son's coffin, and was sure that Nathalia Mikhailovna would react the same way. Something completely unforeseen happened, however. She categorically refused to allow us to the coffin. My argument that it was essential for getting her son the justice she had so desperately sought for the past few years fell on deaf ears. She thanked me for providing her with testimony that her son died because of the actions of a few wicked people, rather than through carelessness, but she rejected exhumation because she did not want, did not dare, to disturb her son's peace. Our conversation took place by the white marble monument marking Zhenya's grave. A photograph of this handsome young man, who should have lived a long and full life, watched us talk.

I was asked by the first deputy of the attorney general of the USSR, Aleksandr Mishutin, to report on the Myasnikov case. Criminal law allows for exhumation to be performed without the consent of relatives, but no one proposed taking this course. It was impossible to go to court, however, without forensic evidence. It was decided, then, to take a pause and hope that Mrs. Myasnikova would eventually give her consent.

But she never did. To this day, the state archives store the closed file on Myasnikov's death. In the end, justice was not served.

# The Kamyanets-Podilskyi Years

# 6. The Forbidden Zone

## *The City above the River Smotrych*

Kamyanets-Podilskyi is an ancient Ukrainian city in the Podilia region. It has beautiful natural scenery, a rich and turbulent history, and is divided by the River Smotrych into old and new towns. The old town is a nationally recognized historic site. At almost every step, there's a plaque that says: "Architectural monument, protected by the state." And famous throughout the country is the city's old fortress and connected museum.

The old town has been an attractive location for numerous film productions. The best known is Alexander Askoldov's 1967 film *The Commissar*, which was banned for twenty years. The locals were thrilled to see the crew's stars, Rolan Bykov, Nona Mordyukova, Raisa Nedashkovskaya, outside or in restaurants. In the old town's market square there was a large banner; on it, was a curiously worded call for "men and women of both genders" to try out as extras. And so the town's residents—of both genders—flocked to the set to make some money and bask in the glory of silver screen.[14]

In the new town, along the steep rocky cliff above the Smotrych River, there is a large botanical garden, a forest, and parks. Back then, I could probably have drawn a map of those cliffs. As a detective in the district attorney's office, I had to climb up and down them countless times, peering into

View of Kamyanets-Podilskyi Castle, early 1960s.

every little bush after dead bodies were discovered on the rocks at the bottom. Lives were shattered against those cliffs for a variety of reasons—drunkenness, murder, suicide.

An incident once occurred in front of law enforcement's very eyes. A criminal, who had raped a sixteen-year-old girl in the park and then thrown her off the cliff, was apprehended. When he was taken to the crime scene to identify the spot at which he committed the murder, he suddenly ran to the cliff edge and jumped into the abyss . . . Perhaps it was the best thing he'd ever done in his life. Once again, I had to clamber down the rocks, examining every nook and cranny, only this time I was looking for evidence of a murderer's suicide.

But I digress. It's just my mind's imprinted so deeply with these cliffs and its rocks.

In the middle of the city's Park of Culture and Rest, as it was then called, there was a dance floor—the park's main attraction and source of revenue. Five nights a week, youth from all corners of the city flocked there to mingle and dance to the thunderous music. There were many of these kinds of dance floors—in parks, clubs, factories. There's hardly anyone among us—we're all grandparents now—who didn't dance on one when we were young.

## *Thunder in a Clear Blue Sky*

In the mid-1960s, the park's director was Grigory Gelbein. About fifty years old, of average height, thin, with a long silvery mustache, he was considered a decent, simple, and lively man. But suddenly—like thunder in a clear blue sky—Gelbein was arrested. OBKhSS operatives, that is, the financial police, took swift and silent action. As soon as the night's entertainment was over, two men dressed in civilian clothes approached the dance floor and arrested two park employees—a cashier and a ticket inspector, both female. In their possession were found counterfeit tickets and part of the evening's takings. It didn't take long for the women to confess that the money came from embezzling from the shooting range. A ticket for dancing was forty kopecks; a shooting ticket was ten. By changing the prices on the tickets and selling bogus ones they had made a profit of thirty kopecks per ticket. They told the police that they'd been doing this for a while at the director's behest and passing all the profits to him.

This latter detail was tremendously important. Petty theft by lowly employees had quickly escalated into a crime at managerial level, with Gelbein, a Jew, as the main culprit. What did this mean in those days? Cultivated and encouraged by the authorities, antisemitism was blossoming in the Soviet Union. In Ukraine, in particular, it fell on ground made fertile with the blood of hundreds of thousands of Jews, murdered throughout history, from the Khmelnytsky Uprising to the pogroms of the civil war. The whole of society was saturated with antisemitism, including law enforcement.

One after another, in different regions, there were major financial crime trials in which most of the defendants were Jews. This inflamed the antisemitic imagination of law enforcement and their fantasy of finding gold, foreign currency, and valuables in Jewish homes.[15] Gelbein was suspected of hording treasures too, but, lo and behold, the police didn't find anything. His case went to the city attorney's office, then, where it fell into the hands of a senior detective: yours truly.

### *"Not on a Whim"*

A policeman brought Gelbein to my office and left the two of us alone. I'd only known Gelbein for a short while; we'd met a few times when I'd done question and answer sessions in the

Grigory Gelbein, second from the left.

park about law enforcement. Still, I had a difficult time starting the interrogation. I was upset by the fact that this smart and well-known person had cooked up such a primitive scheme. As if sensing my unease, Gelbein offered to help me: "Don't give yourself a headache," he said, "I'll tell you everything."

It was true: dance floor tickets were forged on his orders and Gelbein received all the money. But he did not keep it; he gave it all to the city's party committee. He was regularly summoned there by the divisional heads and secretaries who needed funds for various events. Gelbein's arguments that the park couldn't help was dismissed. The money was needed for putting up banners, paying a soccer coach, receiving foreign delegations, anything the party committee thought of in their benevolent wisdom! "So, as you can see," Gelbein said, "I committed these crimes not on a whim, but solely to satisfy the party's will."

I entered Gelbein's testimony, in all its sordid detail, into the interrogation minutes, and we signed them. He was taken back to his cell and I sat in my office thinking about what he'd told me. Slowly, I started to grasp what I'd stumbled upon. I immediately conveyed my findings to my chief and, without waiting a moment, he called the regional attorney's office. They halted any further investigation and told me to report to them the next morning. Why? What had happened? Why were they so on edge?

Goldis in his office, Kamyanets-Podilskyi, early 1960s.

## *The Forbidden Zone*

The creation of an organization which stood above society, the law, and the state was perhaps the greatest "achievement" of the Soviet political system. This organization was, of course, the Communist Party or, rather, its official bodies, from central to local committees (I refer you to the Golder case). These bodies formed a forbidden, untouchable zone, especially for law enforcement, which legally had the power to charge, arrest, or put anyone in this zone on trial. The consequences of breaking into the forbidden zone might change, but there was always a wall in place.

At the annual meeting in the Khmelnytskyi region's attorney's office, a high-ranking party functionary was always present and was always the last to speak. The length of the speech was unlimited. This time it was Levchenko, the second secretary of the region's party committee. He did not stand at the podium, but walked commandingly up and down before us. "You know, comrades," he said, "the party committee has heard that certain attorneys and detectives are trying to charge Communists for criminal offences without permission from the party authorities." He did not elaborate any further, but simply wagged his forefinger and said: "You better beware . . ."

The audience was silent, but suddenly a soft voice came from the back: "What about the constitution, where it's written that all citizens are equal before the law?" The party boss's finger stopped moving. After he regained his composure, he pronounced firmly: "And what does the constitution have to do with it?" From the distance of all these years, I think that if a monument were to be erected to the Communist Party of the Soviet Union, those words should be engraved on it: "And what does the constitution have to do with it?"

I reported Gelbein's case to the region's chief attorney. There was nothing to report, really. The case was not complicated. But there was a problem. Local party committee officials would have to be questioned and a confrontation between them and Gelbein would have to be arranged; but the officials would deny everything.

The summoning and questioning of witnesses was regulated by the criminal law of Soviet Ukraine. But who needs the law when you're a party bureaucrat? The chief attorney traveled to Kamyanets-Podilskyi, then, to discuss the possibility of questioning committee members with the first secretary of the party committee. The first secretary gave his approval, since the crime was before his time. And so I was allowed to question all the functionaries of the city party committee—all of them, except for Tonkocheev, the former first secretary and now the first secretary of the district party committee. His current position had a higher degree of untouchability, you see.

The party functionaries gave their testimonies and said what I expected to hear: they had no conversations about money with Gelbein and received no money from him; and they repeated their claims, and with the same confidence, when Gelbein was present. I reported this to the chief attorney, his deputy, and the head of the detective unit. For all intents and purposes, the matter was closed. The only thing left to do was evaluate the material we had and reach a verdict. Basically, there was Gelbein's testimony and that of the functionaries. Who were we to believe?

I insisted that Gelbein's story was true. He could not have made it up. But I was firmly told that I had no proof and that I was simply relying on my intuition. Why should we believe Gelbein instead of responsible party officials? Why not conclude that Gelbein concocted a clever story to deflect his guilt onto the regional party committee? I was sent back home with instructions to charge the park's director and his subordinates with a criminal offense and report in the coming days about wrapping up the case and passing it on to the court.

### *Invading the Forbidden Zone*

I don't remember exactly when it happened. Was it on the way home from the meeting with the chief attorney, his deputy, and the head of the detective unit, or was it during the sleepless night that followed? Whenever it was, an idea took over my mind which by the morning had become obsessive.

After I got to work the next day, I called the office of the first secretary of the district party committee, the aforementioned Tonkocheev, and asked him to receive me in his office. He said yes, and I rushed to the party committee headquarters in the old town. As I passed buildings bearing historic preservation signs, I realized that I had no permission to encroach upon the forbidden zone. I knew that I had to stop, but my legs stubbornly carried me forward.

Sitting behind a small visitors' desk in Tonkocheev's office and telling him about Gelbein's case, I felt anxious and agitated, afraid that he would interrupt me, tell me to stop wasting his precious time, and command me to get out. However, he listened to me in silence and then said: "C'mon, stop worrying. Gelbein told you the truth. There's no question about it. The comrades in the city party committee shouldn't have behaved like this, but they didn't pocket the money, did they? They used it for the city. Why worry? So they wanted for our soccer team to advance. That would be good for the city—the games would be interesting and people would pay to see them. A good coach is needed—and he needs a good salary—but where are you going to get the money? They had no choice. They had to ask Gelbein. And the same goes for meeting the delegation from Bulgaria. They're our friends—they have to be treated well. But where are you going to get the money for the food? Again, go to Gelbein for help. That's how it is."

As I was listening to Tonkocheev, I thought about how often life provided surprises in the most unexpected of places and at the most unexpected times. When our conversation concluded, I should've thanked him for his time and left. Instead, I told him that I was prohibited from questioning him and that I now wanted his permission to include the minutes of our conversation in the case file. Tonkocheev agreed.[16]

I slowly walked back to work, passing the buildings and their historic preservation signs again. I knew the trouble that awaited me for breaching the forbidden zone and speaking with Tonkocheev. He'd essentially invalidated the charges against Gelbein. But my anxiety was supplanted by a feeling of satisfaction and quiet joy for the rare good that I had been able to accomplish that day.

A plaque in honor of Grygoriy Tonkocheev in Kamyanets-Podilskyi.

As I expected, my bosses expressed distinct displeasure over my invasion of the "holy of holies." I declared Gelbein's case null and void in light of the lack of criminality in his actions.

# 7. "Seven Forty"

Many years ago I fell in love with a dance melody I heard for the first time at a Jewish wedding. They call it "Seven Forty." A strange name, isn't it?

In 1974, I worked as a deputy district attorney in Kamyanets-Podilskyi. Among my responsibilities was representing the district in court. One time, I was preparing a hearing pertaining to malicious hooliganism. An inebriated young man had assaulted patrons in a restaurant without any reason. The evidence was rock solid: we had the testimony of victims, witnesses, medical experts, and, finally, the perpetrator's admission of guilt under the burden of indisputable facts. Everything was crystal clear, except for one detail...

I turned again to the man's biography: Mikhail Khanukovich, twenty-one years old, a student at a construction community college and, as printed on the infamous fifth line in his passport—a Jew. I was flummoxed. In all these years, I'd come across many types of hooligans; they were usually uneducated and primitive people. This was the first time I'd seen a Jewish man of this unfortunate type. Khanukovich's victims were also hardly ordinary—they were well-known and respected people in town. One of them, Faraonov, was the head of the local committee of culture; and the other was Kazimirchuk, a director of a pharmacy. Both were, of course, members of the party. Khanukovich was tried by the district court and his prospects looked very grim—he was facing a sentence of four or five years in prison.

A community center in the city park, where the hearing was held, filled up with spectators. The young man's defense attorney, one of the best in the region, was my old close friend.[17] I was also on good professional terms with the judge: he was experienced and fair.[18] He read the closing indictment and asked the defendant if he pleaded guilty; but Khanukovich answered that he pleaded innocent. I felt bad for the boy. He'd decided to try this useless old tactic in the face of incontrovertible evidence; he was asking for more trouble.

The court proceeded to question the victims. They were both of average height and muscular. Studying them, I wondered how the puny Khanukovich had managed to overpower these strong fellas. Their testimony was precise and reserved, as one would expect from such important people. They'd stopped at the restaurant for a drink after a long day at work. While Faraonov, the culture boss, was talking to the conductor of the restaurant's orchestra about an upcoming performance at a nearby kolkhoz, the drunk Khanukovich charged at them, knocked Faraonov down with a fist to his face, and then clobbered Kazimirchuk who had rushed to help. The police were called and the delinquent was pacified.

The judge gave Khanukovich an opportunity to admit his guilt, but he declined and proceeded to tell his side of the story. He and a bunch of other students were at the restaurant, celebrating the end of final exams. Khanukovich went up to the conductor and asked him to play "Seven Forty." With slight irritation in his voice, the judge interrupted the defendant. "What does 'Seven Forty' mean?" he asked. Khanukovich said it was a Jewish dance and continued his testimony. When he asked to play this dance, Faraonov, who was standing nearby, said to him: "You dirty Jew—you should move to Israel where they'll play your Yid dances for you." In response, Khanukovich struck Faraonov, and then whopped Kazimirchuk, the cavalry.

The community center went silent—so silent that I could hear the drumbeat of my heart in my chest and in my ears the familiar, beloved melody of "Seven Forty." But this was a court and I was the attorney. I turned to the victims and asked for their response to what they had just heard. They both looked at me with an undisguised surprise: "It should be clear to the comrade prosecutor that this is a lie, invented by the defendant." They answered the same way to the defense's questions.

The judge reminded Khanukovich that he had admitted guilt before the trial and had never mentioned "Seven Forty." Khanukovich answered that he didn't trust the detective and had decided to tell the court the whole truth.

Goldis on the right, defense attorney Fillip Kramer on the left, and Judge Anatoly Mitskevich in the middle.

As the court questioned the witnesses—the restaurant's musicians, waiters, patrons—none of them mentioned the conversation between Khanukovich and Faraonov. Indeed, it could very well have been that they simply hadn't heard it. There was one witness, though, who couldn't make the same claim: the conductor who had been talking with Faraonov right before Khanukovich hit him. He needed to state unequivocally that the conversation had or had not taken place.

The judge understood full well the significance of this testimony. He seemed perturbed. I had never discussed antisemitism or anything Jewish with him and could only guess what his feelings on the matter might be. I did know, however, what the government's official position regarding this matter was: there was no antisemitism in the Soviet Union; any statement to the contrary was Zionist and imperialist slander. Thus, as I'd learned from other cases, antisemitic incidents could never be mentioned in official proceedings. This was the reason for the judge's distress. A representative of the state, he had to live up to his stature and question this crucial witness himself.

The conductor's last name was Ukrainets (Ukrainian)— and he was, in fact, Ukrainian man, as well as a bit over thirty and a worker at an auto plant. An amateur musician, he had put together a small orchestra that played evenings at the restaurant. The judge looked approvingly at Ukrainets and said, approvingly: "You work hard and in the evening to help others relax, correct?" The witness, flattered by this praise, nodded his head and smiled bashfully. It turned out that he had never met Khanukovich before, but he did know the victims well and was particularly friendly with Faraonov, who organized the orchestra's performances in kolkhozes. This was precisely what Faraonov wanted to discuss with him that evening. The judge asked whether he had seen Khanukovich hit Faraonov and Kazimirchuk, and Ukrainets said yes.

The judge looked pleased and asked Ukrainets to describe the defendant's behavior. And so the man did: "The orchestra was playing. Faraonov came up to discuss the orchestra's next trip to the kolkhoz. Khanukovich came up as well, offered five rubles, and asked us to play 'Seven Forty.' Faraonov put his hand on Khanukovich's shoulder and said, 'You dirty Jew, you should move to Israel and request your Yid dance there.' Then Khanukovich hit Faraonov in the face with his fist and Faraonov fell. Then he hit Kazimirchuk, who'd come to help."

I marveled at the sheer simplicity and genuineness of the human soul! This important witness did not understand, or did not want to understand, what the honorable judge needed him to say.

It was quiet in the community center, but in my head I again heard an unknown orchestra playing the beloved melody. The malicious hooligan Khanukovich was gone. Instead, there was a proud Jewish kid who had defended his human dignity. Now I understood how he, so puny, had overcome these strong fellas. He knew why he hit them.

But what about me? How many times was I humiliated and dishonored just for being a Jew? And did I hit them in their hateful mugs? Did I say "How dare you!" to any of them? Thank you, my fellow Jew, for giving me this lesson.

After the trial, I slowly walked home, the melody of "Seven Forty" still playing in my mind. What a truly marvelous dance! To this day I don't know why it's called "Seven Forty." But does it really matter?[19]

# 8. A Mistaken Object

This was a collective complaint. Twelve people, who were working as contractors building a cement plant in Kamyanets-Podilskyi, informed the city's chief attorney that their supervisor, the construction and installation foreman, Nikolai Rozbam, assaulted a member of their group, Aleksandr Deryabin. Rozbam found some fault in his work and proceeded to beat him savagely and relentlessly. When he was finished, he, as they put it, "threw the barely alive Deryabin to our feet as if he were a piece of dead game." The forensic examination attached to the complaint left no doubt that Deryabin was indeed the victim of a violent assault.

The twelve workers were furious: they demanded that their rabid supervisor be criminally charged and harshly punished. Theirs was not merely an expression of grievance, but a cry from the heart. Therefore, the chief attorney decided not to carry out a preliminary investigation. He immediately started criminal proceedings against Rozbam according to article 166 in part 2 of Ukraine's criminal code—abuse of power by an official, accompanied by violence. This was a serious crime, which carried with it a severe sentence.

I knew Rozbam from before this incident. He did not look stereotypically Jewish; his last name was not explicitly Jewish either; and his first name was absolutely not Jewish. How had he ended up with the Russian name Nikolai? Perhaps, like so many other fellow Soviet Jews who'd gone from Abram to Arkady, among men, and from Khaya to Raya, among women, he'd switched from Nukhim to Nikolai (later, after emigrating, many made a point of going back to their original names). Who knows whether this was what had happened to Rozbam; what was certain was that he was Jewish and made no secret of it.

My acquaintance with Rozbam was strictly formal. When he was in his twenties, he used to frequent dances in the city park, where he would get involved in the punch-ups that often broke out there. People would get arrested and would usually be charged, but Rozbam had only ever been called on as a witness.

My attitude toward him was complicated. I didn't like it that a Jewish guy repeatedly got involved in drunken fights. At the same time, I couldn't help but admire his bravery, youthful exuberance, and athletic appearance. After he stopped going to

Nikolai Rozbam, early 1960s, Kamyanets-Podilskyi, Ukraine.
Photo courtesy of Nikolai Rozbam Jr.

the dances, I lost sight of him. Now, years later, he was in front of me once again: a thirty-year-old adult and still athletic and handsome. This time, though, he was no longer a witness: he was accused of a serious crime.

It was hard to investigate such cases. Officials who perpetrated assaults would always come up with a robust defense. In fact, not only would they refuse to admit any responsibility, they would also exert strong pressure on their victims and any witnesses to change their testimonies. Rozbam was an exception, however. He did not pressure his subordinates to change their statements and he confessed to assaulting Deryabin from the start. Additionally, he offered new information and asked us to verify his testimony—which we did.

The cement plant in Kamyanets-Podilskyi was built by criminals, whose prison terms were changed to forced labor by the courts. A trailer park was set up near the plant construction site for these "free" men. Their freedom, however, was limited: they could not quit their jobs, leave the trailer park, or break the work schedule. There were all kinds of characters among them; some were natural leaders and some were more obedient. Aleksandr Deryabin (or Alik, as his buddies called him) was clearly a leader: smart, quick thinking, and decisive. He was also more educated and more physically fit than the others. The fact that he was a convicted murderer helped in making him an unquestionable boss.

The convicts (*zeks*, as they were referred to in the city), faced a delicate situation. Suddenly, they were in possession of a freedom which presented all sorts of temptations: women, dancing, restaurants, etc.—everything that youngsters obviously desire. To make these temptations a reality they needed money, which, of course, they did not have.

Despite the fact that the cement plant was of federal importance, its construction was proceeding badly and slowly because of the perennial lack of construction materials and poor management. The workers' pay was minimal as well. In general, foremen and managers would often cheat the system by massaging the number of hours worked in order to increase their men's wages. This would prevent them from quitting. Nothing like this was possible at the cement plant construction, however, as the convicts were not free to leave. That's the point of forced labor. The issue debated by Alik Deryabin's group was how to up their wages without increasing their workload—and their leader finally came up with an idea.

The speaker in Vladimir Vysotsky's famous song wanted to become an antisemite, but didn't know who the semites were. He got an explanation from his "friend and teacher, a local drunk, / who said that the semites were simply Jews." Just like in the song, Deryabin announced to his fellows convicts: "Guys! He's just a Jew!" The men looked at him bewildered. "What don't you understand, idiots?" Alik continued. "Our foreman, Rozbam, is a Jew! Get it? Just an ordinary little Yid. We can break him in two seconds. These Yids are cowards—they're like bunnies. I've seen them..."

They sat around a table and put a plan of action together. The aim was very simple: tell the foreman to raise their pay by faking the number of hours worked. If he refused, they'd threaten the little Jew with violence. No one doubted that the plan would work. The convicts looked admiringly at their leader, and the operation was scheduled to take place during lunch break to make sure that there'd be no witnesses.

A few days later, the twelve workers surrounded Nikolai Rozbam near one of the unfinished buildings. Everyone was silent at first, testing their victim's patience. Then Deryabin stepped forward and said: "We got to talk, boss." He made his proposal, describing his comrades' lives in the most pitiful terms, but Rozbam's answer was a categorical no. He explained that he was not going to break the law.

With peaceful negotiations at an end, Deryabin said: "Listen, Hymie..."

"My name is Nikolai," Rozbam interrupted him.

"I don't know what they call you and why you're Nikolai, but you're definitely a Hymie. We're not going to ask nicely...," Deryabin continued.

He reminded Rozbam that he was encircled by murderers, rapists, thieves—crème de la crème of the criminal world. Then he said: "You have to do what we tell you, or else we might lose our temper."

"I see that," Rozbam answered. "But what about fairness and decency?"

The crew stared blankly at their ringleader. "I got you," Deryabin said. "You want to keep this hush-hush. No problem—it'll go in the vault."

"No, what I mean is that there are twelve of you against one. You think that's fair?"

The "Twelve Apostles" were confused for a moment, but the ringleader soon regained his composure. "You want to go against one of us? Fine, that might be better. Pick anyone you want. But remember—you'll have to do what we tell you when it's over. Those are our conditions."

"I have two of my own," Rozbam replied. "We won't do it here. There's a quiet place I know—and it'll be one against one. I can't have fights at work, especially not with my workers. I value my job; I have a family. And my second condition is: whatever happens, there won't be any complaints or reports!" Nikolai Rozbam looked at the men surrounding him, pointed at Deryabin, and said: "I'll fight you. You seem to be the one in charge..."

"Are you so frightened, Hymie, that you've completely lost your marbles? You understand what you're saying, right? I can 'accidentally' beat you to death, you know..."

"So you're saying no?" Nikolai asked.

At this, Deryabin agreed to Rozbam's conditions.

They decided to fight in the unfinished building's cellar. The two combatants went down the stairs, and the others waited outside, eagerly anticipating their leader's quick and inevitable victory and the fulfillment of their demands.

After ten or fifteen minutes, Rozbam slowly came back up the stairs, breathing heavily, and carrying a bruised and bloody Deryabin in his arms. As the convicts stated in their complaint—and correctly—Rozbam dropped their defeated idol at their feet. "The lunch break is over," he quietly muttered. "Clean him up and get back to work..." Then he walked away. The convicts were stupefied, unable to utter a single word.

There's a term in jurisprudence: a "mistaken object." It refers to when criminal picks an object (or a place or a subject), studies it with some nefarious purpose in mind, but ends up with something he didn't expect. Imagine, for example, a thief who sneaks into a room containing a safe, cracks it, but finds useless papers instead of wads of cash inside. Or a rapist who follows his victim, but when he grabs her in a dark alley it turns out that he's dealing with a long-haired man. Etc., etc. The law calls for punishment in "mistaken object" cases.

This was Deryabin's and his gang's mistake. They chose a Jew as their object because they'd thought Jews were weak. That's the lie their environment had fed them their whole lives. But they tangled with someone very different—a kind of Jew they didn't know existed. One who was strong in body and spirit; a man with pride and guts.[20]

# 9. Twenty Years Later

## *The Worst Is First*

I graduated from Kyiv State University in 1953 and was dispatched to the Stara Ushitsya district—the most godforsaken and remote part of the Khmelnytskyi region—to serve as a detective in the district attorney's office. All the knowledge I acquired before now seemed completely superfluous: the theory and history of state and law, Roman law, Latin, and other intellectual fancies. I'd get real crimes now. In the 1950s, the police did not have to carry out preliminary investigations; all cases and incidents were dealt with by a detective in a district attorney's office.

Goldis on the left in Stara Ushitsya, Ukraine circa 1956.

A few months into my new job, I began to investigate the case of one Ivan Kuvilo, who was accused of physically abusing and "moderately" injuring his wife. He was arrested and pleaded innocent. It seemed like yet another instance of the very common crime of domestic abuse. Husbands and wives, in-laws, neighbors, etc., often resorted to fists or whatever they had in their hands to resolve quarrels. The results were broken noses, jaws, arms, legs, and ribs—all classified as moderate injuries.

The nature of my relationship with the culprit, or rather his relationship with me, was set during our very first meeting. Kuvilo was a bit older than me and our life experiences were drastically different. He quickly figured out that I was an untested detective and a timid intellectual. He was surprised by my politeness during questioning—"Please, tell me," "Please, explain," I'd say—and laughed at it. Having spent most of his life in prisons and penal colonies, he was not used to a detective treating him like this. He was used to ruthless masters.

He began to see me as an oddball, even a weirdo, and became increasingly rude and defiant. While I always addressed him with the polite "you" (*Vy*), he invariably responded with the familiar "you" (*ty*).

"Could you tell me, please, when and why you were in court?" I'd ask.

"I wasn't," he'd reply, giving me a mocking smile.

"But your wife testified that you . . ."

"That bitch will say whatever gets into her head . . ."

Such were most of our conversations.

The investigation was completed, and I needed to familiarize the accused with his file. And I had to do this in the prison where Kuvilo had been transported after being held at police headquarters.

The prison was located in the city of Proskuriv, the regional center, which would be renamed Khmelnytskyi just a year later. After arriving in town, I stopped by the detective division of the regional attorney's office, where I was told that I shouldn't have spent so much time questioning Kuvilo about his criminal record. I could have simply requested the information from the region's department of internal affairs. I stopped by the department and within minutes had Kuvilo's entire criminal record in my hands. I was amazed. He'd first been tried at the age of sixteen. By 1953, he'd had five previous convictions!

Having informed the regional attorney's office about Kuvalda's conduct, I was told to give him his file in the presence of a prison guard; but my request for one was denied by the prison's chief warden. He said that if I was afraid to be alone with the felon, I should have him transported to the attorney's office. The prison had no staff for such "niceties." I took offense at this suggestion and replied, stifling my wounded pride, that I'd see Kuvalda on my own.

Kuvilo sat across from me in his cell. I informed him that the investigation was over and that he now had the right to read his file. "Get on with it," he said, graciously permitting me to begin going through the documents with him.

"Page number 1: A declaration to initiate the criminal proceedings..." I read.

"Why the hell do I need to listen to that? Move on," he interrupted.

"Your wife's testimony..."

"That snake should go fuck herself."

Somehow I was able to reach the last page despite his constant commentary—the file I'd obtained from the department of internal affairs. But then something happened so quickly and unexpectedly that it took me some time to realize that the file's whole contents were scattered all over the floor and shredded into little pieces. And now Kuvilo was lunging at me with a massive stool raised above his head, the very stool he'd been sitting on and which, for whatever reason, wasn't bolted to the floor as prison regulations stipulate. In front of me was a desk; behind me was a wall with a barred window; and I didn't have a weapon on me, as prison rules forbade bringing them in.

What happened next can only be described with one word—fate. As I learned later, after I arrogantly left the chief warden's office, he started to think over his decision to refuse me a guard. He ordered one to go to the floor where I was meeting Kuvilo, and to check on me from time to time through the cell's peephole. My lucky stars aligned at the exact moment Kuvilo came at me with the stool: the guard was just looking through the peephole. He threw open the door and jumped at Kuvilo like a goalkeeper trying to block a shot. The guardian and Kuvilo fell onto the floor, as did a stool, with a thunderous racket. Other guards ran into the cell, and within a few minutes Kuvilo was in handcuffs. They saw that he was chewing something and extracted a few pieces of his criminal record from his mouth.

Before the prisoner was removed from the cell, he looked me up and down with scorn and shouted: "Remember, you fucking egghead. I'll find you. I'll get you from under the ground!" Left alone with the pieces of what used to be the criminal case file all over the floor, I slowly started to grasp what had just happened. By not reacting to Kuvilo's insults during the investigation, I'd done a disservice not just to him, but to myself as well. He'd been confident that I was a greenhorn he could wrap around his finger. The fact that I'd diligently written down his lies about his lack of previous convictions had convinced him that he'd have no problems with me. But when he saw his criminal record in the file, he became furious and violent. As far as he was concerned, all my politeness had been in service of a plan to prove his recidivism.

And all of this happened during my first ever visit to the prison walls! Worst is first, as the folk wisdom says. Indeed! I put the remains of Kuvilo's file in my briefcase, put the stool back into its place, and, with my spirits crushed, headed back to the attorney's office. There, however, I was greeted as the hero of the day. Not just the detectives, but the attorneys, too, came to gawk at me and the destroyed file. Nevertheless, I was still reprimanded for all my lapses in judgement during the investigation.

I was given an office for the night and left by myself with the scraps of the file, some pieces of paper (both regular and transparent), some glue, and a pair of scissors. I pushed all the office furniture into one corner, spread everything on the floor, got on my knees, and crawled around on them for the rest of the night. By morning, I was able to present a mutilated, but more or less repaired, file. The only intact document in it was the ill-fated summary of Kuvilo's criminal record! Once again, I presented the prisoner with his file, but at the attorney's office this time and with two policemen with me. Kuvilo was quiet and did not interrupt me, but his occasional side-glances in my direction reminded of the promise he'd made me in the prison cell.

In the end, I didn't worry too much about the recidivist's threat, even though his time behind bars had turned him into an impulsive psychopath. He was in prison again and would stay there for a long while. This was what everyone thought—

except for my boss, the district attorney of Stara Ushitsya, Maria Lebedeva. She was unnerved by what had happened and insisted that I resign immediately and move somewhere else or request a transfer to another district or even region altogether.

I did neither, of course, and stopped thinking about the incident, absorbed in the new adventures of my detective life. Little by little the new cases, meetings, and problems pushed it out of my mind. With the passing years it became a blur and some sort of an apocryphal tale. Yet God works in mysterious ways . . .

## *A Silent Agreement*

It was 1973—twenty years since the start of my career and graduation from university. I was now a deputy city attorney of Kamyanets-Podilskyi. There were two attorney offices in the city—city and district. Everyone was in the same building and the two branches were tightly linked both professionally and personally. Thus, there was nothing unusual when the district attorney stopped by my office and asked for a favor. A house in a village in the district had to be searched. None of his subordinates were available to do it and he did not want to stoop to such a "lowly" assignment himself. He gave me a warrant and provided me with a car.

I read the warrant. The apocryphal tale of long ago had become a reality: I had to search Ivan Kuvilo's house. It turned out that he lived in the village of Krushanivka, a place I knew well from my years of working in the Stara Ushitsya district. I asked the district attorney about Kuvilo, and his description confirmed my fears: it was the same person. I was about to meet the man who'd almost killed me once and had promised that he would finish the job one day. But I wasn't particularly concerned: time really does seem to heal all wounds.

It hardly needs mentioning that searches are one of the most important investigative procedures and that, if carried out professionally and on time, they can yield a lot of evidence for solving a crime. There are, however, searches that are undertaken without any specific goal in mind, but for purely formal reasons, that is, to avoid future accusations that some steps in the investigation were skipped. The search I was about to perform in Kuvilo's house was precisely such a formal procedure.

The district police officer, who accompanied me, invited two of Kuvilo's neighbors to serve as witnesses. So we all entered the house together. I do not know whether I would have recognized my old acquaintance had I not known that it was him. After all, twenty years had passed. His manners, however, were very familiar; his glances in my direction also clearly signaled that he recognized me. We both knew who each other was, then. Yet, by some unspoken agreement, we acted as if this was our first encounter. Perhaps it was to be expected, considering how we'd parted twenty years before.

Since the search was a pure formality, the officer who was supposed to assist me quickly lost any interest in the job and sat lost in boredom. He frequently stepped outside for a smoke or dozed off at a table. The witnesses were also equally passive. Sitting indolently together on a bench, they looked around, patiently and silently waiting for permission to leave. In other words, I was the only one actually working.

When the search was almost over, I stopped by the door that led to a space I had not yet examined. The door was locked. I asked Kuvilo where it led, and he responded that it went into a pantry. In response to my request to unlock it, he said that there was nothing there, just some old junk. Used to scrutinizing literally everything in a house during a search, I insisted that he open it. He hesitated for a bit, then found the key and unlocked the door.

We entered a small space, which indeed looked like a pantry. However, there was no junk anywhere. Instead, right in the middle, there was a moonshine machine in the process of making "poison." According to Soviet law, producing moonshine was a criminally punishable offense. How this law was enforced is another story—it would require much more than a short memoir.

Thus, I, an attorney, was a witness to a crime. I certainly knew what I had to do and had done multiple times over the previous twenty years; this time I decided not to do anything, however. A silent agreement seemed to have been reached between Kuvilo and me, as if some invisible puppet master was in control of our actions. Neither he nor I uttered a word, realizing that there were people on the other side of the door who could overhear us and come in. We communicated with each other in silence, only our eyes conveying our thoughts.

My interlocutor's eyes did not ask for anything, did not plea for mercy or forgiveness. He peered straight at me with a bit of a mockery, as though saying: "Well, prosecutor, I'm in your hands again. So, fine, go ahead, pay me back for the evil I once did to you . . ."

"No," he should have read in my eyes. "It's because you're now in my control that I won't harm you . . . I don't want to answer evil with evil . . ."

Such (or almost such) was our silent dialogue next to the illegal device, the moonshine machine. It didn't last long, and a few minutes later, we left the pantry, again without uttering a single word. I announced that the search was over, sat down at the table, and wrote in a protocol: "Nothing was found or confiscated during the search." I won't lie—when I wrote those words and read them aloud, I had the feeling that the officer, for whom the discovery of a moonshine machine would have been a great professional achievement, would get up and make me come clean. He'd take the key, throw open the door to the pantry, and reveal its contents to everyone. But nothing like that happened . . . All the search participants signed the protocol without any comments, and I handed a copy to Kuvilo.

I was about to leave and bid goodbye to Ivan Grigorievich. Again, just like in the pantry, he was intently staring at me. This time, I read in the eyes of this once mettlesome and inveterate recidivist, now an exhausted man, beaten by his unlucky life: "Thank you very much . . . Do not be sorry for what you've done . . ." I would never see him again.

# 10. A Defendant's Oral Argument

Even for such an inexperienced detective as I was at that time, this case presented no challenges. Nikolai Ostrovsky, the manager of a village store, received a substantial sum of money from the authorities to purchase produce. He bought nothing and embezzled the money. There was plenty of evidence against him and he did not deny his guilt.

The investigation proceeded quickly and smoothly, and was about to be wrapped up, but as always (or almost always) happens with criminal cases, there was a hitch. Something inevitably pops up to complicate the things and make a detective's life challenging. When all I had left to do was present Ostrovsky with an indictment and his file, he stopped responding to my requests to come to the district attorney's office. There was another complication, too: the store was in a village in the district I worked in, Stara Ushitsya, while the defendant resided in Kamyanets-Podilskyi, about fifty kilometers away. Furthermore, because he was handicapped from the war, it was decided not to arrest him. The case, however, needed to be completed and by a certain deadline at that.

I put Ostrovsky's case materials in my briefcase, grabbed a couple of packs of cigarettes, and set out for Kamyanets-Podilskyi. When I arrived, a local policeman took me to Ostrovsky's house, which was located in the old town. As I walked along its picturesque side streets and lanes for the first time, passing by the many impressive ancient structures, I had no idea that in a decade or so I would constantly traverse the city's old and new sections.

Assuming I'd catch him at home, I hadn't made an appointment with Ostrovsky. His entire family was there: his wife, whose unhappy face bore traces of her hardly sweet life, their daughter, an attractive nineteen-year-old student at the city's teacher college, and their son, a tenth grader. Everyone was there, except for the person I needed. I'd messed up. I introduced myself and explained the purpose of my visit. The wife said she had no idea where her husband was. She painted a picture of a drunkard who was hardly ever at home. I asked her to inform him that he must report to the district attorney's office at once. Annoyed with myself, I left Ostrovsky's house with nothing.

The workday was over. The bus for Stara Ushitsya had already left, and there was no way I could get back home. Mind you, it was a bus in name only. It was a truck covered with tarpaulin and a few benches in the back. There was only one hotel in town, and it was impossible to get a room without reservations, so I had no choice but to stay the night in a detective's office and sleep on his desk. Such comfort was nothing new to me: many nights in my district, I'd had to sleep in village council halls and kolkhoz offices on desks and chairs, stranded there after work. So I covered the detective's desk with newspapers, took off my jacket and shoes, and put the briefcase containing the accursed file under my head. Tossing and turning on this unbearable surface, I somehow managed to fall asleep.

Everything that happened later defied all logical explanation. At two o'clock in the morning, I woke up and it was as though I split into two people. Half of me got up, turned on the light, and put on my jacket and shoes; the other half whispered, "Stop it . . . What do you think you're doing? Have you lost your mind?" I did not heed my inner voice and went outside. It was a magical winter night: all was quiet, the sky was crystal, and the snow squeaked pleasantly under my feet.

Suddenly, my legs took on a life of their own and carried me toward Ostrovsky's house, even though I'd only been there once before. Logic dictated that I should have gotten lost in the narrow, twisty little side streets of the old town, especially in the dark. But I walked in the right direction and stopped in front of the right house.

I knocked on the door. There was no answer. I knocked on the window. After a few wearisome minutes, the door opened and I saw Ostrovsky's son standing on the threshold. "Please, call your dad," I told him. "He's not home," the boy answered. "Didn't we tell you in the afternoon that he never comes home . . ."

Obeying some kind of sense, but certainly not common sense, I stepped past the boy and into the dark house. I recognized the layout: a small hallway, a kitchen, and then a room. There was no door separating the kitchen from the room—only a doorway from which curtains hung. I stopped in the doorway and saw, in the darkness, two people lying on the bed by the opposite wall: the mother and the daughter. Trying to be as calm as possible, I apologized for the intrusion and again, just like in the afternoon, asked the wife to tell her husband to come to the attorney's office. There was no response.

I realized that the women, who were certainly awake, did not wish to speak to me. All I could do was withdraw.

Suddenly I felt (not saw or heard, but *felt*) that there was someone behind the curtain. Only now did I start to feel fully conscious, and I realized I was in quite a predicament. It was clear that the person I was looking for was behind that curtain. Hiding from me, and hence from justice, he'd been drinking and wandering around town. What could I expect from such a man? And behind me there stood his son, a strong fella, who'd lied to my face about the father's absence. The danger I faced was obvious—plus no one knew I was here, all alone, at night.

My preservation instinct, accompanied by fear, kicked in from head to toe. I didn't have a weapon on me (a year before there had been a government ordinance forbidding attorneys from carrying weapons, and we'd had to turn our guns in). What could I do? Turn around, push the son away, and run? But my stubborn feet wouldn't shift. Trying to overcome the shakiness in my voice, I uttered, "Well, Nikolai Evstafievich, I've come to pay you a visit and you're hiding in your own house... Please explain yourself..."

The curtain barely moved as Ostrovsky emerged from behind it. He was wearing riding breeches, boots, and a shirt. Without trying to conceal his displeasure at my late night call, he barked at me, angry and irritated: "What the hell do you want?" In truth, all I wanted at that moment was to get out of this darkness and run away. I could hardly admit that, though. I told him that I urgently needed to discuss his case with him, but that it'd be better to do so outside so as not to disturb his family. He put on the army coat he still had from the war, placed his hat on his head, and we went outside.

Breathing in the clean, cold air, I felt elated that I'd escaped the hole I'd dug myself into. My fear was gone. Now the man standing next to me didn't seem like a bandit capable of anything; my anger toward him subsided. Once outside, Ostrovsky also changed; his aggressiveness and coarseness were gone. His shoulders drooped and he transformed before my eyes into the man he really was: a pitiful loser. The frosty air turned out to be good for both of us. We talked for a while in his front yard, and not just about the case. Then we started to slowly walk back toward the attorney's office.

Sitting behind the desk on which I'd been trying to fall asleep a couple of hours earlier, I presented the indictment statement to Ostrovsky. He pleaded guilty and we began to study the file. Sometime later, he went back home while I, sitting behind the same desk and unable to doze off, contemplated the night's bizarre events that had brought the investigation to its conclusion. I gave the case materials to the chief district attorney and he sent them to the district court. New crimes and cares lay ahead of me.[21]

The Stara Ushitsya district attorney's office had a minimal staff. There was only an attorney and a detective. Therefore, if the attorney could not represent the district in court, for whatever reason, or simply did not feel like doing it, which also happened, the detective—me, in other words—had to take his place. From early on, then, I started to acquire court experience, which came in very handy when I became the deputy district attorney in Kamyanets-Podilskyi and was largely responsible for representing the district in court. As you might recall, the district attorney of Stara Ushitsya and my very first boss was Mariya Lebedeva. In Ostrovsky's case, for whatever reason, and probably without any explanation, she decided to send me to trial in her stead. Of course, I had no need to prepare for the court proceedings, since I knew the case through and through.

Ostrovsky's wife and children sat in the courtroom and the hearing went along without any complications. All criminal court proceedings consist of three oral arguments: the first is by an attorney, the second by a defense council, and the third is by the defendant (he gets the final word). In most cases, defendant statements tend to be very brief. They mainly boil down to a request for acquittal, if the defendant pleaded innocent, or a request for leniency, if the defendant pleaded guilty.

Ostrovsky's defense council was a young lawyer who would go on to become my close friend (he would participate in the "Seven Forty" hearing). He had just begun making his oral argument when Ostrovsky suddenly stood. He put his hand on his defender's shoulder and said: "That's enough. Thank you, kind sir, for standing up for me, but now please sit down and listen to what I have to say . . ." The defendant's behavior was so unexpected, and ran contrary to all the established norms, that everyone was flabbergasted. No one, not even the masters of the courtroom—the judges—interrupted or stopped him. We all listened to his speech in silence.

"My defense council said here that I'm a good man because I fought in the war and have a nice family. And he asked you to take pity on me. And comrade prosecutor said that I embezzled the state money and have to bear responsibility for it. Yes, it is true. But neither the defense council nor the attorney said the most important thing about my crime. I squandered my life, threw it away. I destroyed my self-respect through drunkenness and laziness, brought sorrow to my wife and shame to my children. I, a reconnaissance officer, who stared death in the face many times at the front, stooped to running away from this detective, like some delinquent. I don't deserve any pity from you. I have to be punished in the toughest way possible, which is exactly what I'm asking you, esteemed judges, to do." Thus, the defendant delivered his oral argument as his own prosecutor. It was a unique situation, and I never saw the like again in my long career in court.

The court heeded Ostrovsky words, but did not satisfy his request. The judges realized that he did not deserve a strict punishment. He received the minimal penalty, which did not include any prison term.

# Women

Throughout my many years as a detective and then a district attorney, I invariably met many women. A great majority of them were victims of various crimes, but a few were involved in criminal activities themselves. Yet no matter who they were—victims or defendants—they shared one distinct quality: they experienced their suffering much more intensely than the men I dealt with, be it as anguish resulting from being beaten or misery from the harsh living conditions of prisons and camps. But their suffering was not only physical, since, as is well known, women are capable of withstanding such hardships much more courageously than men. I was most disturbed by the moral agony and affront to their dignity as women, which shook their spirit. It was difficult to witness that. This is perhaps why I was always especially struck by those cases in which women were able to overcome their terrible circumstances and rise above their problems. The episodes in this section tell these women's stories.

# 11. Valya-Valentina

A district division of the Ministry of Education received a brief, yet ominous and anonymous, letter which said that a teacher in a secondary school in the village of Kulchyny was involved in a sexual relationship with a tenth grade female student. The division's inspector, Leonid Papernyi, was tasked with investigating the matter. Like most Jews who worked in official Soviet organizations and institutions, he was a conscientious worker. This job was extremely demanding, since the letter mentioned no names and he had to do his work without impugning or offending either the teachers or—especially—the female students.

Papernyi was able to work out a plan of action for this delicate situation. Upon arrival at the school, he informed the principal that the Ministry of Education wanted to carry out medical checkups on the female students. Accordingly, all the girls from the tenth grade were sent to the local gynecological office, where Papernyi asked the obstetrician, as if just in passing, to note whether any of them were not virgins. Out of the twelve students, two turned out to be sexually active. The inspector spoke with them in confidence right after the exam. One student said that she was involved with a local guy, whom she loved and intended to marry. The other admitted that she was sexually involved with a gym teacher. Thus, within just a few hours, the anonymous letter was verified and its information confirmed. Of course, no attorney, fenced in by the walls of procedural norms, would have dared to act like Papernyi did. The results of his inspection shocked the authorities: a serious immoral incident had been uncovered, and it involved one of the school's best female students.

Her name was Valentina, Valya for short, but her friends called her by her full and short name at once—Valya-Valentina. She was the best in everything: an A student, involved in extracurricular activities, and head of the school's Komsomol branch. She was also beautiful and morally upright, truly the pride of the school.[22]

The district division of the Ministry of Education transferred the materials of their inspection to the district attorney's office to determine the teacher's culpability. As a detective, I got answers to certain standard questions which always arose in such situations. The main question was whether a rape took place and whether the teacher used his position to force the student into the affair. The investigation had to be carried out discreetly so that no one in the village or at school, or even the girl's family, would learn about it. Thus, I instructed the district division of the Ministry of Education to call in the teacher and Valya separately on the pretense of discussing, with him, the upcoming athletic competitions and, with her, the upcoming meeting of the leaders of school gardening teams. Both of them came at the requested time and were sent right away to the district attorney's office.

Investigations of sexual crimes have a number of specific peculiarities and problems. The first of them is how to question the victim. While the detective wants to obtain the most detailed testimony possible, the woman, especially an inexperienced young woman, might be reluctant to reveal them. Humiliated both physically and morally, she might feel ashamed and uneasy about relaying such information, especially to a man. As a result, young women tend to provide yes and no answers.

Valya-Valentina behaved in precisely this manner. It became clear from her yes and no answers that there was no force involved, either physical or psychological, and that everything happened and continued to happen fully consensually. She and the teacher loved each other and wanted to marry as soon as she graduated. My detective's soul felt uneasy. There was no rape, no coercion. There was simply love between two young people, and it had nothing to do with law enforcement. There was only one more thing to do—get the teacher's explanation and close the case.

His name was Viktor Ivanovich. He was twenty-five years of age—the best age, as the Romans used to say, as the naivete of youth has gone but all of life remains. A discharged sailor, tall, fit, and broad-shouldered, he was an extramural student in the Athletic Department at the pedagogic institute. When questioning him, I kept on singing in my head the words from the song of my youth: "To Saratov/ to Saratov/ to his native hearth / a blue-eyed sailor / just returned from Kroonstad."

The arrival of such a guy at a village school was, of course, an extraordinary event. He was constantly surrounded by the romantically minded, older female students, who looked at him with adoring eyes, ready to fulfill his wishes. His choice fell on Valya-Valentina for her combination of beauty and intelligence. He was cautious and decided that it'd be better to deal with a smart girl, who'd be able to keep their affair a secret. However, as is well known, it's hard to keep a secret anywhere—and even more so in a village. I asked Viktor to briefly describe, on paper, his relationship with Valya. He looked at me in disbelief and asked what I had in mind, as intimate relations between a student and a teacher were out of the question. The unease quickly left my soul. I was about to have a difficult conversation with a man who was denying the obvious.

I informed him that Valya had told me everything about their secret. Viktor looked at me reprovingly, but calmly, as if I were a gullible student, and began to explain what was right and what was wrong. How could anyone seriously believe that he, a teacher and also, by the way, a party member, would permit himself to become sexually involved with a student? What Valya is saying ... Well! These are simply the fantasies of a young girl who has picked me as her hero and is now concocting stories!

I invited Valya back into the office and told her that Viktor had denied any intimacy between the two of them. She sat, her head hanging, staring at floor, and asked Viktor, without changing her pose, whether he had indeed denied everything. She listened to him, her head still hanging, as he kept on saying, in a calm and patronizing tone, that all girls get caught up in romantic fantasies, but that there had to be a limit. Nothing had happened, he said. He respected her as an excellent student and a good friend, but he could not let her ruin his reputation as a teacher and party member.

When he finished, Valya asked me if she could tell him something. I nodded and suggested that I leave to give them privacy. She asked me to stay, however. I felt the poor girl; she'd just been dealt a devastating blow by the man she loved. And it wasn't just a blow to her personal life: her faith in the very possibility of beautiful and genuine love had been rocked. I was afraid that Valya would have a nervous breakdown. What happened next, though, is the reason I decided to record this case for posterity.

Valya-Valentina raised her head and straightened her back. The fragile girl, dumbfounded by the deceit and betrayal of the man she loved, was gone. In her place there sat a proud and calm woman, confident in herself. She asked the man sitting across from her to listen carefully and look her in the eyes. And then she proceeded to speak. A metamorphosis took place before me. I don't want to try to replicate their conversation, and not because so much time has elapsed. It wasn't what she said that mattered, but how she said it. It was the speech of a woman who had conquered her sorrow, got up from a blow that had just knocked her to the floor, and learned at the very beginning of her life's journey the true meaning of what two people can say to each other.

With each of her words, Valya reconstructed for the teacher the history of their relationship and explained why she had believed his promises. Another metamorphosis was taking place. This discharged sailor—tall, stout, handsome, and confident—was turning into an average nobody. He fidgeted in his chair and his eyes darted around the room; he had discovered that Valya was not some immature teenager, but was an independent woman who dared to reveal the truth about their relationship.

Viktor was afraid to acknowledge the truth, as he didn't know the law and thought that he could be charged for having sex with a minor. So, in an attempt to evade responsibility, he made a surprising decision. When Valya stopped speaking, he forced a smile onto his face and said that he had listened to her with the utmost attention. He could not corroborate what she had said, he announced, since nothing had taken place; but he did see that she was a very smart and decent person who would be a faithful and caring wife and that, therefore, he would be happy to marry her. He was sure that Valya would gladly accept his offer; after all, he knew how much she loved him.

But Valya said she had no desire to marry him and that she rejected his offer. A seemingly simple, naive village girl had the upper hand and would not forgive his lies and betrayal.

When the teacher left and we were alone in the office, Valya told me that she was four months pregnant and did not want to have this dishonest and phony man's child. This was a very serious problem. According to the law of the time, abortions were only allowed within the first three months of pregnancy. Terminating pregnancy after this period was permitted only in extreme medical circumstances, determined by a special medical board. In the absence of such circumstances, a late abortion was considered a crime. This meant that if I, a detective and officer of the law, helped Valya get an illegal abortion, I would be an accomplice to a crime. At the same time, I felt that I had no choice but to help her, and comforted myself with the fact that the law could not take into account the full complexity of people's lives.[23]

I turned for assistance to my colleagues in the city attorney's office in Khmelnytskyi; they made sure that the abortion would be done in the regional hospital there. I don't know what they said to the doctors, but a few days later I got a phone call from them to tell me that Valya could go to the hospital.

In order to justify her departure and the absence from home for the next two or three days, we concocted a story that she would be visiting the nearby kolkhozes with the leaders of various other schools' gardening teams. And on the day of her appointment, I drove Valya to the hospital in the district attorney's official car to have the abortion.

About two weeks had gone by when the secretary came into my office and told me to turn on the radio. There was a report about the regional conference of the leaders of school gardening teams, where Valya was speaking. I turned on the radio. In her usual resounding voice, Valya-Valentina was giving a speech about her team's work.

# 12. Samara

*1.*

I got lucky. The emergency, my very first case as a detective, wasn't a mysterious murder, or a theft, or a rape. It was an "ordinary" suicide. In a village, a woman, living alone, had hanged herself at home. I still felt very anxious, though. Rather than do a training exercise, I was required to investigate an incident that had actually happened. I wouldn't be looking at a mannequin; it would be a real person hanging dead from a rope this time. And I'd have to make independent decisions.

I carried a detective's suitcase, packed with all sorts of objects that were useful when working at a crime scene. Its contents were truly diverse: a hammer, scissors, pliers and tweezers, all kinds of measuring instruments, devices for taking fingerprints and footsteps, and much more. The most important item in the suitcase was, of course, a camera.

It's hard to overestimate the importance of photographing the site of an incident—photos immortalize the event. Therefore, while approaching the dead woman's house, I was frantically trying to recall the rules of photographing the scene of a crime which we were taught in the forensics seminar. First, I had to make an overview shot, then a midrange picture, and finally, a detailed shot.

Goldis (with his back on the right) on assignment, circa 1956.

At the site, I was accompanied by the head of the village council, the district police inspector, and two witnesses who stood respectfully aside. With a slight trembling in the knees, I started to do the job. I examined the front yard, the house, and the body, all the while taking photos—overview, midrange, detailed—ready to use all the film I had in the camera.

The examination was over. Satisfied and relieved, I went out into the front yard which, as I expected, was filled with onlookers. I'd just taken a deep breath of fresh air and lit a cigarette when a boy of about twelve years old came up to me and politely asked: "Mister, why didn't you remove the cap from the lens, when you were taking pictures? . . ." Later, whenever I went to a crime scene for the nth time, I always recalled this unfortunate bungle so that I'd never again forget to remove the cap from the lens. And just like the first time, when doing a new job I was always filled with anxiety.

## 2.

That is exactly how I felt when I left for yet another emergency with a group of police detectives and forensic experts. In a village, an assistant to the head of the kolkhoz had been murdered in his own house. The murderer was unknown, which intensified my stress and feeling of responsibility. The murdered victim lay on a cloak tent raincoat spread out in the middle of the living room. We knew that he had a big family—a wife and seven small children. When we began to examine the site, the children stayed with their mother, who was breastfeeding in another room of their big house.

The dead man lay on his back with blood all around and under him. His head was almost split in half. As was the rule in such cases, we began to propose various theories about what might have transpired. After carefully examining the victim's head, the forensic expert declared that he must have been struck once, very forcefully, on the head a single time, most likely with an ax. It was logical to conclude that only a physically very strong male could have delivered such a blow. This view was obviously important for initiating a search for the murderer. All the physically strong men in the village had to be accounted for and their potential link to the murder investigated.

Just as we were animatedly discussing the next steps, we heard a quiet female voice behind our backs. We turned around to see that it was a slender, petite woman, the victim's wife. "No," she said, "that's not what happened. There wasn't any man here. I killed my husband . . ." We looked at her with surprise and undisguised disbelief. She silently exited the room and returned after some time with the murder instrument in her hands—a bloodied ax. The search for the murderer was no longer necessary...

## 3.

In pre-Soviet times, there was town on the River Volga called Samara; the Soviets renamed it Kuibyshev. A Ukrainian guy by the name of Fyodor did his military duty there. He also fell in love with a local girl and, after discharge from the army, took her to his native village, Orlyntsi, located in the Podilia region. Her name was Tonya, but someone once called her Samara, and the nickname stuck. Tonya didn't mind it and eagerly responded to the nickname, since it reminded her of home.

Fyodor had a sharp wit and was a hard worker, both at home and in the kolkhoz. He became an assistant to the head of the kolkhoz and built a big lavish house for his family, which quickly increased in size. They had seven children: the oldest daughter was fourteen and the youngest son just ten months old. Tonya took care of the house and Fyodor helped her in his free time.

Tonya adjusted quickly to the new place; her cheerful and sociable demeanor came in handy. She and Fyodor seemed happy. Yet, one could not but notice that Samara started to lose weight and look older than her age. Was there anything surprising in that? Many village women aged prematurely because of the incredibly strenuous work they did and their harsh living conditions. Be that as it may, Tonya was losing weight and aging for other reasons, and she desperately tried to hide them from others.

Fyodor was not merely sharp-witted and a hard worker; he was controlling and domineering. He was pleased with his wife, but did not like it that she loved her freedom. He wanted her to be servile, treat him like her master, and defer to him in everything. She, however, would only settle for equality. Fyodor's decision was to force her into obedience. Once a month, drunk, he would beat her after finding fault in some trifle. The violence increased and became regular, gradually turning Fyodor into a home despot.

Tonya put up with this cruelty for the sake of the children and his relatives. She did not tell anyone about her misery, no one heard her complaints; she tried the best she could to explain away to curious neighbors her multiple bruises and bumps. The happy family was long gone and its place was taken by Tonya's incredible patience in the face of this horror; only the children and her love for them helped her weather her husband's violence.

Once, during yet another brutal episode, which Tonya was again ready to endure in silence, she saw a sharp razor in her husband's hand, got frightened, ran away, and hid in the vegetable patch for a few hours.

It was soon time to feed the baby. Tonya left the vegetable patch and headed to the house. Her oldest daughter, who was aware of everything, of course, greeted her on the porch. She said that her father was napping inside. Tonya walked into the house. She had to get the cookies that were in a cupboard in the room where Fydor was napping on the floor so that she could dissolve them in the baby's milk. She tiptoed into the room and approached the cupboard.

Suddenly, Fyodor grabbed her by the skirt, pulled himself to a sitting position, and pulled Tonya down to the floor with him. He did not yell or grow violent, but spoke quietly and slowly without losing control. "Why," Fyodor asked, "did you leave the house and hide from me? Did I ever injure you or break, God forbid, anything? Never. Nothing. I only give you these little shake-ups to keep you in line. You know that. Why, then, would you leave the house and hide? I never expected something like that from you, Samara. I'm your master and you must obey me, but instead you ran away. For this you must be punished."

He turned Tonya so that he was looking at the back of her head, took out the very same razor out of his pocket, and cut off her braid in one quick swoop. Then he proceeded to slice her dress. Finally, he turned Tonya to face him and started lightly drawing the blade over her face and breasts. "See," he kept saying, "if I press just a bit you'll be gone . . . I'm not going to do it now, but one day, when I feel like it, I will . . ."

All this time, Tonya had been silent and motionless. She did not feel any pain. While he was speaking and holding the razor in his unsteady hands to her throat, her life with this man rushed before her eyes, her life with the guy she'd once loved, the boy who'd had soft, curly hair when she'd first met him; she saw her life, full of horrendous labor and endurance, unfathomable physical and moral suffering. "Look here, Samara," she heard, as if from a distance, "no more joking around. Now go and make supper . . ." Fyodor folded the razor, put it away in his pocket, and stretched out on his raincoat on the floor.

Tonya quietly got up, went into the barn, picked up an ax, and, just like before, tiptoed into the room where Fyodor was lying. She lifted the ax and brought it down on her husband's head. She packed everything into this single blow: all the pain she felt for her lost happiness, all her torments and suffering, and her blind hatred for the man who had destroyed their life together. That was why this petite woman's strike was equal in strength to that of a powerful man.

The forensic expert confirmed Tonya's testimony about the injuries on her body and the cuts on the dress.

## 4.

Fyodor was a native of Orlyntsi and had many relatives in the village. Tonya, who moved there from the Russian heartland, had no one. There were fears that Fyodor's relatives might do away with her to avenge his death. The first few days were especially worrisome—during the funeral and the wake, when people's grief was inflamed by the exorbitant drinking. So, to protect her, we took Tonya and her baby away from the village.

She returned home after three days, accompanied by some policemen and me. We decided to tell the villagers about the results of our investigation. The auditorium in the village community center was overflowing with people. Tonya was here as well. I relayed everything you've just read—a sad story of destroyed love. I showed photos of the cuts on Tonya's neck, chest, and dress. I also showed Tonya's severed braid.

The audience was silent, taking in all the horror of what Fyodor had done. Fyodor's older brother stood and stated on behalf of his entire extended family that no one would touch Tonya and asked her to stay in the house. He then went up to her and said, "Please, Samara, don't leave your house, live in peace and raise your and Fyodor's children. We'll help you . . ." The people in the audience started to cry. The detective couldn't hold his tears either.

**5.**

The trial found Tonya "culpable of her husband's murder due to the strong emotional agitation prompted by the victim's criminal actions." She received a purely symbolic conditional sentence. The court's verdict was never appealed.

# 13. Nadezhda Petrovna

*1.*

Soviet criminal law provided for a greater accountability for crimes committed by groups of people. Naturally, the actions of people, united by a common criminal intent, pose a greater threat to the state and society than the actions of individuals. The law distinguishes between various types of collective crimes. There are temporary groups that arise spontaneously in certain situations. Consisting of two or more people, they usually commit one or two crimes (murder, hooliganism, theft, etc.) and cease their activities. There are also more organized groups—gangs and criminal rings—which work together longer and commit large financial crimes (theft, robbery, burglary). They can also include officials involved in bribes and embezzlement.

There was a criminal group operating in Kamyanets-Podilskyi that was atypical, however. Its five members pursued a single goal—gang rape. Their main objective was not sex, though, of which they had plenty, but the mockery and degradation of their victims. The group's organizer and clear leader was a twenty-three-year-old called Sergei Svidersky. He taught his accomplices that they should have no qualms about their actions: women were put on the earth precisely to fulfil the gang's aims.

The gang needed apartments where they could drag their victims. They would find them with the help of acquaintances and friends who would let them use the space for a few hours. Only Svidersky hunted the victims and brought them back to the various apartments.

He was a handsome guy, could put on a friendly smile and speak eloquently, and had no problem persuading women to join him. He had many ploys, depending on circumstances. For instance, he would stand near a major shopping area with his girlfriend, Zhanna, who knew about everything and helped him lure victims, and someone else from the gang. Svidersky would pick out a young woman, introduce himself and Zhanna to her, pretending to be Zhanna's boyfriend, and invite the unsuspecting victim back to the designated apartment to have dinner, listen to some music, or play cards. Zhanna's presence always quelled the women's misgivings. Flattered by the attention of a handsome, friendly, and by all appearances decent guy, they gladly went along with their new friends.

The rest would happen according to a well-polished scenario. Alone with the woman, the smile now gone from his face, Svidersky would order her to undress. The woman's surprise and protestations would cease after two or three slaps in the face. Then Svidersky would explain the situation, letting her know that she would leave the apartment alive and well only after satisfying all five guys in the apartment. Then, depending on his mood, he would either stay with the woman or leave and give permission for his buddies to start in the order he'd previously established. They had absolute freedom to do as they pleased with the victim. She would be frozen with shock and terrible fear.

The naked woman would be photographed alone or with the gang. Svidersky would also make sure that everything looked natural, with her smiling and looking at ease. This was done so they could blackmail her should she complain or confide in someone. The women were also threatened with violence. Thus, not a single victim dared to come forward with any information about what had been done to her.

Before letting the victim go, the gang would surround her; each member would comment disparagingly on her looks and behavior while she, like a hunted animal, had to listen to these monsters. The women who went through this ordeal would later experience a nervous breakdown, from which they had to recover on their own. In other words, they maintained their silence. Sometimes they would bump into someone from the gang on the street and run away in desperation. This, however, was unnecessary, since none of them were any longer of interest to Svidersky and his accomplices. It was that first time that was important—when the victim was totally helpless.

Everything that I'm now writing here was the subject of a detailed investigation and later the trial, when Svidersky's gang was uncovered and put behind bars.

The case was tried by the regional court while I was the prosecuting attorney. There were eight victims in total. They provided a detailed testimony about the torments and humiliations they went through, as the defendants sat in silence, their heads lowered. The court's verdict was justly severe. The leader of the gang was sentenced to fourteen years in prison; the rest also received lengthy prison sentences.

This was a famous case. Everyone involved in its successful resolution—the detective and the police—was praised and received financial awards. The region's chief attorney separately noted my "skillful" representation of the district in court. All of us, however, who took part in the proceedings and were now applauded by our bosses, forgot how we had managed to uncover this gang which threatened the lives of the city's women for more than a year. We forgot about one person, without whom there wouldn't have been either the sensational revelations or the triumph of justice. This person was a woman, after whom I've named this story—Nadezhda Petrovna. She knew neither the victims nor the defendants, and was not part of law enforcement. She was an ordinary worker in the textile factory.

I recall seeing a few years ago an experiment on television that was filmed by a hidden camera. A man lay on a sidewalk on a busy urban street. He seemed to be well and healthy. People would rush past, paying no attention or at best giving him a side glance, but no one stopped to make sure that the man was OK or needed help. I encountered a lot of human misery through my work and can attest that much of it could have been avoided had it not been for bystanders and their indifference. As the Ukrainian proverb says, "My house is by the roadside—I know nothing."

## 2.

Sergei Svidersky was especially happy that day. He'd "delivered" to his gang an innocent seventeen-year-old girl called Lena, who'd come to the city from the far provinces to attend the culinary college. Everything was going according to plan. When her ordeal was over, Svidersky decided to give his friends, who were getting drunk in the nearby apartment, a gift. He called them and said that there was "fresh meat" which he would now bring over. All the rapists left, except for Svidesrky and one other gang member. On the way to the apartment, they explained to Lena that she would need to spend some time with the new men.

It was late autumn, around six o'clock in the evening. Svidersky gave Lena her coat so that she could cover over naked body. He also let her have her boots back. But nothing else. Threatening her once again with violence and reminding her about the incriminating photos, Svidersky, his buddy, and Lena left the apartment.

Along the way, Svidersky realized that he'd forgotten to take his camera and went back to get it. Lena was left with the gang's cruelest member, whose nickname was Kyrgyz. Svidersky knew that Lena wouldn't be able to escape from him and that she was too terrified to try anyway.

Nadezhda Petrovna was slowly walking home from work on the opposite side of the street on which Lena and Kyrgyz were waiting for Svidersky. Tired after another tiring and noisy day at the factory, she was carrying a string bag—so common during Soviet times—packed with groceries that she'd inevitably obtained after she'd spent ages standing in a long line at a store. Nadezhda Petrovna saw a young man and a young woman were standing around on the other side of the street, but there was nothing unusual about such a sight.

However, she could tell that the woman was frightened, and that the man was holding her wrist rather than her hand. An unconscious sense of alarm shook Nadezhda Petrovna. If it had been one of those TV experiments, she wouldn't have ignored this scene, so she stopped and called out to the girl: "Hey, what are you doing here so late? Your parents must be worried sick waiting for you. Go home now! Don't you recognize me? It's Aunty Nadya!"

There was no reaction. Lena continued to look at Nadezhda Petrovna with the same frightened glance; Kyrgyz was also silent and gripped Lena's wrist even more firmly. Without thinking about what might happen, Nadezhda Petrovna crossed the street, went up to Lena and Kyrgyz, took the girl by the arm and said, "Didn't you hear what I said? Go home, right now!" She then turned to Kyrgyz: "Why are you holding her wrist like that? You can see her tomorrow. Or do you want me to call the police?" Kyrgyz had no choice but to let Lena go. The two women then left. All of this lasted no more than a few minutes.

When Svidersky got back, he saw that Kyrgyz was by himself and that some woman was walking with Lena into the distance. He was furious—but there was nothing he could do about it.

Nadezhda Petrovna took Lena home with her and invited her to take off her coat. The young woman started to cry hysterically. Nadezhda Petrovna saw that the girl wasn't wearing anything under her coat. She calmed Lena down and then listened to young woman recount the horror she'd experienced that day. Nadezhda Petrovna gave Lena some clothes and they went to the police station. The young woman made a detailed statement about what had happened, what the rapists looked like, and the names and nicknames she'd overheard. She also showed the police where the crime had taken place. By the next morning, the entire gang was behind bars.

And what about Nadezhda Petrovna? After leaving Lena in the hands of the police, she returned home to her daily cares.

# 14. Alla

*1.*

This was promising to be a very significant case. Implicated were regional commerce employees who were involved in selling new and used cars and taking large bribes in the process. Their accomplices were employees of the state motor vehicle department, who forged documents for the car sales when needed. The thread of criminal connections reached all the way to the top, to the regional party and the state authorities and their bosses.

A case of this magnitude called for an equally high level of investigation. Thus, the office of Ukraine's attorney general created an operative group, which included detectives both from attorney offices and police department from various regions. I was among them.

The investigation was headed by Mikhail Zakharchenko, the detective responsible for the most significant cases in the attorney general's office. He was a highly skilled and brilliant man, an independent thinker and quick and impulsive when making decisions. Of average height, thin, darkhaired, and with dark eyes, he could have been taken for either a Ukrainian (which he was) or a Jew... For some reason, however, everyone called him the gypsy. The nickname stuck so well that whenever his bosses needed to summon him, they would yell to the secretary, "Bring me the gypsy!"

To be a Jew in the Soviet Union was to be a marked person; those who tried to hide their Jewish identity were in an even more precarious position. Someone from among Zakharchenko's "well-wishers" drew the attorney general's attention to the fact that he looked and carried himself suspiciously like a Jew. Plus his name was also Jewish-sounding—Grigory Mikhailovich! This was a serious insinuation. So one day, the attorney general summoned Zakharchenko to his headquarters and dryly asked him, in front of all his deputies and without reverting to the bigoted nickname: "Grigory Mikhailovich, as a conscientious attorney and a Communist, tell us, in all honesty, who you actually are. According to your passport, you're a Ukrainian. But why lie? You look like a Jew and everyone also calls you the gypsy. So who are you really? Please give us an honest answer..."

Zakharchenko looked obediently around the room and answered, addressing the attorney general: "Fyodor Kirillovich! I understand that this is a very serious matter and will answer truthfully. I cannot spread falsehoods in front of such an esteemed audience." He paused for a second and then said: "Here's my story. First, the gypsies gave me to the Jews in exchange for clothes, and then the Jews sold me to the Ukrainians for gold!" Everyone was silent. Not knowing how to react to these words, all the deputies anxiously awaited their boss's reply. A single word from him would decide the whole matter. The attorney general did not wait long to respond: "What a sneaky scoundrel you're, gypsy! Why don't you go to hell." And thus, the "investigation" of Zakharchenko's Jewishness was over.

## 2.

A central perpetrator in this big, one could even say humongous, case was a young woman by the name of Alla. She was not even thirty when she became the director of the regional car dealership. After a few years of success, praise, and making valuable connections, she was now facing the collapse of her life and career and, most certainly, prison time. At Zakharchenko's directive I investigated the bribes with which Alla was directly involved and interrogated her about them. She denied some accusations and confessed to others. This went on throughout my time with the defendant.

At the end of one interrogation, when I was just about to leave, Alla turned to me with a surprising request: "Would you happen to have forty kopecks? If you do, could you stop by the cosmetics store and buy me some eyeliner, please? Leningrad brand." I was startled. What cosmetics store? What eyeliner? She was accused of a crime for which she could get up to fifteen years in prison or even a death sentence. I was very confused about all this. First, she'd be better off figuring out how to lessen her punishment; second, there were very strict rules about what one could bring a prisoner, and deliveries were permitted only at certain times and with thorough vetting by the wardens; and third, was I really going to run errands for a prison inmate? "Well, do you have forty kopecks or not? Don't worry, my mom will pay you back..."

I didn't say anything, left the prison, and headed to search for Leningrad eyeliner, which I handed to Alla during our next questioning session. This little item initiated a new period in the life of our main subject of interest. She put the crime and all her legal worries on the back burner; her human dignity and, especially, her dignity as a woman in custody moved to the front and center.

I became Alla's accomplice in these matters and continued to fulfill her requests. I didn't go to the stores again, but I passed her requests along to her mom, who would give the items to me or a warden to hand over to her daughter. My relationship with Alla was on a less formal footing; we trusted each other more and would spend hours discussing various topics after our official meetings.

"You have to understand," Alla would say, "no matter how difficult things are, a woman can never forget that she's a woman. Alone in my cell, on my bunk, I start banging my head against the wall, thinking that everything's lost! But as soon as I have to face the public, no one can see the slightest sorrow on my face. I need them to see me as the woman they knew before prison—proud and attractive. This is now much more important to me than my defense against your accusations."

Indeed, as much as prison allowed, she always tried to look her best. Once she even got a wig, but it was confiscated when the wardens realized that the rules banned such luxuries. In response, Alla demanded a meeting with the chief warden in my and Zakharchenko's presence. She explained to him that she was not a fresh army recruit whose head could be shaved; she was a woman with lustrous hair that needed looking after. Should the chief warden provide a way for her to maintain her hair, she would have no need for the wig. But if he couldn't, she would refuse to leave her cell or answer any further questions.

The chief warden saw that she was not joking and decided to cave. "C'mon, Alla, is a wig really worth all this trouble?" he asked her patronizingly and with half a smile. "We'll give it back to you. Wear it to your heart's content!" The man was sure he'd hear words of gratitude, but instead he heard something very different. "I cannot recall, comrade chief, when we decided to switch to the informal 'you.' Please do keep this in mind and convey to your subordinates who always use it with me for some reason..."

The prison staff was quite surprised when they received a directive to address Alla only with the formal "you." "I am a criminal and justly imprisoned," Alla said to me after the meeting with the chief warden. But does that give them the right to humiliate me?"

Alla was not shy about telling me that all commerce managers and directors regularly received and gave bribes, and that it would be like that as long as there were shortages of goods and all goods were distributed from the top. During one of our sessions, she asked me, "Aren't you tired of me yet?"

"No," I answered.

"Well, good, let me read you my poems, then . . ." From then on, Alla always brought a small school notebook with her and read her poems to me. Some of them were satirical and some lyrical . . . quite good overall.

The ten-month investigation was over. All the necessary papers had been completed and signed. The trial loomed. When Alla and I parted, she asked for my advice about what to wear to court. I recommended something very modest and told her that, in the city, she used to provoke other women's jealousy with her fashionable outfits. She thanked me and left.

Sometime later, I received a request from Alla to visit her in prison. She asked me to tell her mom that she needed her black-and-white dress for court. It was one of her favorite and most lavish dresses. "Don't look at me like that," Alla said when she noticed my bewildered glance. "Let the judges add a few more extra years to my sentence, but I want to look my best, the way people are used to seeing me: beautiful and fashionable." And that is how I remember her—beautiful and fashionable, but also a smart and proud woman who was not crushed by life's struggles.

The court sentenced Alla to nine years in prison; she served six. Upon release, she made a stop in Kyiv on her way home. She bought a bouquet of flowers and visited the attorney general's headquarters, where she handed the flowers to her main legal accuser—Grigory Zakharchenko.

# Part Two

# OTHER MEMOIRS

# 15. Serbiyanka

*To the blessed memory of my parents*

"Those who wet themselves—step forward!" The order is addressed to the squadron of telegraphists of the Ninth Reserve Communications Regiment, stationed in the city of Atkarsk in the Saratov region. The squadron consists of four platoons, forty men each. The 160 men of the squadron are standing to attention. The commander is the platoon leader on duty in the barracks. The barracks are a former auto parts storage facility—a long and narrow building with a cement floor. Along one wall stretch countless bunkbeds covered with straw mattresses. The bunkbeds are three-storeyed. The height of each level is about half a meter.

Each morning at six o'clock, an orderly on duty yells in a heart-shaking voice, "Squadron, up!" Within three minutes, each soldier must get up, get dressed, make up his bed, and take his place in the formation. Therefore, after hearing the orderly's harrowing roar, the soldiers jump up, as if scalded with boiling water. Every time, they also hit their heads against the upper bunkbeds, curses flying everywhere.

"Those who wet themselves—step forward!" This command is heard every morning; and every morning, twenty to thirty guys step forward to face the platoon leader. The wet and the dry gaze at each other; there are no smirks, no funny comments. Those who don't step forward today know that they will be the ones in the front tomorrow or the day after. Everyone knows that this happens not because of incontinence, but because their lives consist of constant drills and hunger. Exhausted and starved, the soldiers collapse on their mattresses and are out like the dead within seconds. It's no wonder they wake up covered in urine.

I'm not going to try to describe what we soldiers of the Ninth Reserve Communications Regiment were fed during the war. It's probably best to convey it with the words of the soldiers' saying: "You're gonna live and that's about it." Did that mean that the soldiers were always in the state of doom and gloom? No, not at all. They joked, laughed, even had daydreams. They were all young—and that says it all.

The horses' stable was converted into the platoon's mess hall. With the horses out, a plank half a meter wide was raised on a small column in the middle of the stable. Each pair of soldiers sitting opposite each other at the makeshift table would share a small pot of food. There were no forks and no need for them, but each soldier had to have his own spoon. Therefore, the spoons were all different—some bigger and some smaller, some deep and some shallow.

Mess hall partners who had different spoons would go to see the commander, since whoever had the bigger spoon would obviously be able to eat more of the shared food. If one ate quickly and the other ate slowly, they would have to see the commander, too, and he would pair them with another partner. Again, there were no smirks, no funny comments.

Bread, a large loaf and an additional small chunk, was given out separately to each division thirty to forty minutes before the start of the meal. Three times a day, each division sent their representative to the mess hall to get the bread; he needed to be the most conscientious guy and not devour the extra chunk along the way. Then the ritual of handing out the bread followed: one soldier, the bravest one, cut the loaf into chunks, depending on the number of soldiers in the division. Then, pointing to each chunk with his knife, he asked a soldier who had his back to him: "Who is this one for?" "For Petka," the soldier with his back to him answered. "For Vanka, Grishka," "For me," For you . . ." This ritual ensured fairness.

The most important thing, however, happened next. Each soldier, alone with his portion of the bread, had to leave it untouched for half-hour before bringing it to the mess hall. This required an enormous amount of inner struggle and depended purely on the strength of one's will. Some devoured their bread immediately, without giving it a second of thought; others placed it under their pillows, making every effort not to go near it or even look at it. None of this was new to me. I arrived in the army with an old and intimate knowledge of hunger.

\*\*\*

In July 1941, my mom, my seven-year-old sister, and I were evacuated from Ukraine to the Saratov region and placed in the village of Simonovka in the Durasov district. Mom and I worked in the kolkhoz. By the fall, she and my little sister had moved to Durasov to work in the field hospital while I stayed in the village and continued on at the kolkhoz.

The first months of the evacuation were more less bearable, but the hardships and deprivations of the war gradually reached our remote village. This period, spent in the village, was momentous for me. In Simonovka, having had a carefree childhood, I discovered the meaning of labor for the first time, got to know the life of a village, and learned to respect farmers. For the first and only time in my life, I lived in a place that was completely free of antisemitism. It was just not in the air. The residents of this Russian village did not know what antisemitism was and had no need to learn it.

I lived with the Gusev family. The head of the family was Vasily Arefievich, his wife was Anna Matveevna, and their fifteen-year-old granddaughter was called Nyura; they treated me like a member of the family rather than a temporary lodger. In the evenings, the family would sit down to supper. Anna Matveevna would place a large plate of food in the middle of the table while everyone respectfully took their seats around it. Straightening his mustache, Vasily Arefievich would take the first large spoonful of food and chew it in his half-toothless mouth. Only then could the rest of us take a spoonful—but we had to wait until he gave the start signal. Nyura and I could hardly bear it. We wanted to devour everything in one quick swoop, but did not dare to break the routine.

When the supper was over, Vasily Arefievich would light his pipe and say: "Now you, Mishka, put on your army jacket, take Nyurka, and off outside!" "Outside" meant to go for a walk. Nyurka and I would rush outside, where young men and women were already promenading with their harmonicas and balalaikas, singing the famous "Saratov Blues": "Because of you, the green fir trees, / I'll never see Saratov again, / because of you, the hazel pretty eyes, / I'll have to suffer without end." So many of those ditties got stuck in my head and haven't left.

Afterwards, we'd divide into pairs and groups. We, the fifteen-to-sixteen-year-olds, wandered off to the edge of the village, sit under a stack of straw, and tell all sorts of stories—

although the stories didn't matter. Everyone sat next to whoever they really wanted to sit next to. My place was next to Shura. We sat tightly together, shoulder to shoulder, motionless and barely breathing.

Around 1:00 a.m., Nyura and I would tiptoe into the house, but the still awake and ever watchful Vasily Arefievich invariably greeted us with the same phrase: "Now, you, Mishka, go sleep on the entresol while you, Nyurka, off to the stove."

At five o'clock in the morning, I would already be on my way to the tractor brigade to work on trailers until 7:00-8:00 p.m. every night. Then it was dinner and promenades with Nyura again. Only teenagers can withstand such a regimen.

\*\*\*

I left Simonovka deep in the fall of 1941. By this time, more and more young men, with whom I used to sing the ditties on the village street, were going to the front, with fewer and fewer of them coming back.

Mom and I worked in the city. Since we were an officer's family, we received additional food rations; but it was hardly enough. We exchanged whatever clothes we had for food in the nearby villages. We starved, as did so many other people who left the occupied areas and ended up in places very far from home. Therefore, the state of constant starvation in which the soldiers of the Ninth Reserve Communications Regiment found themselves was nothing new to me; it had been a part of my life as a civilian.

\*\*\*

When I left for the front on November 3, 1943, I did not yet know that I was about to replace my father, Captain Bentsion

Ichilevich Goldis, who had perished on October 12, 1943 in the battles for the liberation of Kyiv. I took his place three weeks later, just like in Vladimir Vysotsky's song: "We barely had time / to look back / as our sons / went into battle."

My father is buried in the mass grave in the village of Lebedivka in the Vyshgorid region, half an hour's drive from Kyiv. More than a thousand warriors who were buried in different places in Lebedivka and nearby areas during the fierce battles on the approaches to Kyiv found their eternal rest there. After the war, the government decided to gather their remains in one mass grave. During the reburial, which was attended by people from the whole region, a priest performed the necessary rites over the dead. Someone from the crowd approached him and said that among the dead there was a non-Christian, a Jew, and pointed to the coffin containing my father's remains "There are no Christians, Russians, or Jews here," the priest said to him in a loud voice. "There are only the sons of the Motherland, who gave their lives for it!" This was said when shameless state antisemitism was sweeping the country.[24]

At the common grave near Kyiv, where Goldis's father, Bentsion, is buried, shortly before leaving for America in 1993. Grinberg is reciting the kaddish.

***

The life of the communications company, like the life of any other army unit, was governed by a strict daily routine. After breakfast, the platoon lined up in the barracks for dispersal. The platoon commander, Guard Senior Lieutenant Alatortsev, gave his instructions and we headed to our designated places. The platoons were formed based on the soldiers' heights. The first platoon had the tallest men, who were called "columns" or "reference points." The smallest, so-called "pencils," were in the fourth platoon—mine.

One spring morning in 1944, after dispersal, the company commander ordered the fourth platoon to remain in the barracks and wait for his return. When ordered, we lined up. In front of us stood the commander and next to him a petite young woman—a blond, with the uniform and the shoulder insignia of a junior lieutenant. "From now on, the commander of our platoon will be Junior Lieutenant Sergienko, Klavdiya Ivanovna. Please assume your command," the company commander said and left.

We stood facing our new commander. During the war, the personnel of reserve regiments consisted of soldiers of different ages. Among us there were twenty-five-to-thirty-year-old men as well as seventeen-year-old youngsters, like me. Naturally, we were all different—culturally, intellectually, educationally—and had different manners. But at that moment, all our differences flew out the window. Forty men with few similarities were united by a single idea which could be summed up with one word: protest. It was a silent protest against the fact that we, as men, refused to be subservient to a woman.

Our feelings must have been plain on our faces, which is why the new commander said: "I hope we're not going to have any issues; don't let it bother you that I'm a woman. I graduated from a regular military academy. I'm an officer. I will do whatever is stipulated by the military statutes. I ask that you only see me as your commander."

My God—was anyone listening to her? A young, attractive woman was standing in front of us, and no power in the world could force us at that moment to see her as anything but that. However, how could we, the soldiers, show her, the commanding officer, that we refused to obey her? One of our ringleaders had an idea: "We won't sing!" This was the first practical step toward manifesting our protest.

Soldiers and song are inseparable. No matter where they're headed—the barracks, the mess, to drills—they sing. At least this is how it was in those bygone years of my army service. Whenever soldiers did not want to sing for whatever reason, a conflict would arise between them and the commander, which would almost always end with the officer's victory. The non-singing unit would be run back and forth, made to crawl until, exhausted, they would begin to sing. The soldiers' obstinacy was always punished.

An assistant to the platoon's commander, Sergeant Alexei Ratnikov, lined us up. Out of all of us, the "pencils," he was the shortest, but also the most cheerful; he liked to find a quiet place in his free time, take his harmonica, and play songs from his native Vologda region. He issued his usual command to start marching with a song. We stepped forward, but no song followed. He stopped and tried again—but nothing. We knew what was going to happen next. They would order us to run—fine, we'll run as far as possible from the girl commander; that will teach her how to handle real men.

Instead of the command to run, however, she ordered us to stop and face her. Fine, we knew what to expect—now she'll start scolding us and threaten a severe punishment. But we heard something completely different: "Don't want to sing?" "Nope, we don't want to." This response came from the red-headed Kostya Mikhailov, the platoon's troublemaker. We waited for the commander's angry reaction to this insolent answer. However, giving us a smile—something we hadn't seen in a long time—she said that these things happened and that she herself could only sing when in the mood for it. Either way was fine.

No one had ever spoken to us like this. We started to feel less confrontational, and slowly but surely we began to recognize the commander in this petite young woman. On the first day we met her, someone from the platoon had called her Serbiyanka, a play on her last name Sergienko. After that we always called her Serbiyanka amongst us.

Soon, it was time for the commander's first night duty. In the barracks, by the entrance, by the wall across from the bunkbeds, there was a small table and two chairs for the officer on duty and the orderly. This was a special duty. One hundred and sixty men slept on their three-storey bunkbeds in the crammed space, which made the air in the room very difficult to breathe. From time to time, soldiers would invariably get up. They were those who could actually wake up when nature called, but hardly any of them managed to reach the toilet located outside. Those who slept by the door would run outside, but the rest would get off their bunkbeds and, with their eyes half-closed, move toward the door while peeing all over the cement floor, as if it were a flower bed. After finishing their business, they'd return, relieved, back to bed. There were worse cases, of course. This was hardly a spectacle fit for a woman, but there was nothing she could do. She diligently served her shift and only covered her eyes occasionally.

At six o'clock in the morning, the orderly yelled: "Platoon, up!" Everyone jumped out of their bunk, curses flew left and right, and then we heard a sonorous female voice issue a command: "Platoon, listen up! This is Commander Sergienko. If anyone had an accident during the night, there's no need to get up and get dressed. Stay in your beds; you'll clean yourselves up after the rest of the platoon leaves!" This is how a young, seemingly inexperienced officer got rid of the humiliating ritual of making the soldiers who'd wet themselves step forward. And after her very first night duty at that! After that day, Sergienko was not just our commander, but the company's favorite officer, and we "pencils" took pride in that. The singing resumed also. People on the street would stop and marvel at the platoon's measured step and the great singing that was inspired by our strict and demanding, but also caring and beautiful, commander, our Serbiyanka.

We knew everything about her. She was only twenty-one years old and was single. We were terribly protective of her and insisted on an explanation regarding every suspicious occurrence, which she tried to provide to us in all seriousness. This protectiveness was not unfounded. When Klava Sergienko had arrived at the regiment, many of the young officers and not so young commanding staff would not leave her alone. She understood the danger of this, so from the very beginning put a stop to anyone's attempt to get close. We knew this, but we still kept a close eye on her.

***

In early June 1944, command exercises took place in the Privolozhsk military district; they were exclusively for the senior staff, that is, the generals. A group of officers and soldiers from our regiment was dispatched to provide communication for the exercises. I was included in this group as a telegrapher and so was Serbiyanka as a switch mechanic. The exercises took place in the territory of the famous Tatishchev military camps, established in the Saratov region during tsarist times.

This was a fairy tale come true—no barracks, no drills, no hunger. A few of us soldiers lived in a cozy room and slept on regular beds. Three Morse code transmitters—one connected with the district headquarters in Kuybushev, another with the headquarters of various armies in Saratov, and the third with some place which masqueraded as the battleline headquarters. The room, bright and clean, also had a telephone exchange installed in it and a small table for the liaison officer. The generals swarmed around us—a huge number of generals. I'd never seen so many before in my life. Literally towering over all of them was the monumental figure of the commander of Privolzhsk military district, the legendary Colonel General Khozin, who was rumored to be Jewish.

We ate the scraps from the generals' table and felt as full as we'd ever felt; we worked on the Morse code transmitters, receiving and sending messages which were dictated sometimes by the generals themselves. It was a clean and relatively easy job. It was for a good reason that the telegraphists were called the soldiers' "intelligentsia." I did not know then that these two weeks as a telegraphist in the Tatishchev camps would be my sole experience with the profession. When our platoon arrived at the front, the receiving major told us: "Forget that you're telegraphists. We have no need for those; you're all to go to the front as line signalmen..."

In the Tatishchev camps, work was around the clock. Whenever I had night shifts, Junior Lieutenant Sergienko was also on night duty as a switch mechanic. We would be alone in the communications room. There wasn't much to do, the generals had no desire to work during the night and enjoyed a reprieve from the war. Serbiyanka and I would sit by the open window, take in the fresh nocturnal air and talk—about everything. At first, I felt constrained; after all, she was my commander and my idol. But gradually I relaxed. We talked and didn't notice switching to the informal "you" and our first names.

There was nothing sexual involved, or even the hint of it. And not because I was still so young and inexperienced. It was because both of us, innocent in body and spirit, seemed to value intellectual kinship and conversation the most. We both loved songs and sang sitting by the open window. We sang quietly so as not to wake up the sleeping generals all around us: "Oi, cornflowers, cornflowers, / There are so many of you in the field. / Often we'd gather them for Olya, / Running to the river beneath."

The two weeks of bliss had flown by, and we had to return to the regiment—back to the barracks, the drills, and the hunger, the ranks and formalities. I walked into the communications room for the last time; Serbiyanka was dismantling the switchboard. I put my hand on her shoulder: "Well, Klavochka, let's get ready." Suddenly, I heard a voice behind my back: "Soldier, approach." This was an officer on duty, a senior lieutenant I hadn't noticed upon entering the room. I reported that I was a private in the fourth platoon of the telegraphists' company, the Ninth Reserve Communications Regiment. "And who is that?" he asked me in an ominously calm voice, pointing to Serbiyanka. I explained that she was the platoon's commander. The officer blew up, "So how dare you, you son of a bitch, treat her like that?" "Guilty as charged," I said, staring at the floor.

The officer, however, was not interested in my remorse. He thought he'd seen the untouchable Klava Sergienko, she who'd refused every single officer's proposition, having some sort of affair with a puny soldier in rags. The officer decided to take his anger on me, yelling, waving his fists in front of my face, and asking for the tenth time how I dared to act like that. I stood silently, only repeating, like a parrot: "Guilty as charged."

Each military regiment had its own inept soldiers, their klutzes. They all had different nicknames; in our regiment, they were called "Tambovers" (from Tambov). To say that a soldier was from Tambov meant that he was an idiot, a moron, not quite right in the head. The senior lieutenant suddenly stopped shouting, looked me up and down, and said quietly, even softly: "Are you a Tambover, by any chance"? "Yes, indeed, comrade lieutenant," I swiftly answered. "Get the hell out," the officer said and breathed out in relief.

***

Back at base, everything returned to its regular course. Klava became comrade junior lieutenant again. Never again did I dare to address her by the first name or the informal "you." I also never told anyone about our night duties in the Tatishchev camps. However, whenever we met on our own, she would call me by my first name and smile to let me know that those magical days, or rather nights, gifted to us during the command exercises, were not forgotten.

Notwithstanding the hunger and drills, the entire fourth platoon also lived a fairy tale thanks to Serbiyanka. She would visit us in the barracks for a while after we'd finished the day's training. She ripped her linens to make forty collars for us, and made sure we sewed them on instead of our old ones, which were full of holes after so much washing. The red-headed Kostya Mikhailov, whom she appointed as her orderly, would hand her his military tunic, needle, and thread and ask to sew on his collar. It's not a man's job, but a woman's, he would say. We'd all laugh, including Serbiyanka, as she sewed his collar on. It seemed she wanted to be our "woman" and not just our junior lieutenant. We even asked her to take off her military robe and put on a dress and high heel shoes for us. And she did.

If one of us was under the weather, she would sit for hours by the sick man's bed, like a nurse. Still, there wasn't any familiarity between us; she was our commanding officer, whose orders we meticulously followed the best we could. Therefore, our platoon became number one in all activities after her arrival. And we thought she'd never learned that among ourselves we called her Serbiyanka.

***

Our term in the reserve regiment came to a close; we were being sent to the front. Serbiyanka and Alexei Ratnikov came to the railway station to bid us farewell. She hugged and kissed every one of us. In that moment, we all wanted to throw away the formalities and ranks, press our faces against her blond hair and say: "Farewell, Serbiyanka!" Yet no one dared to—and that's a shame. When the train began to move and, huddling by the open doors of the box car, we were waving to her, Junior Lieutenant Klavdiya Ivanovna Sergienko shouted out: "Don't forget your Serbiyanka! . . ."

# 16. Above the Abyss

This place is long gone. It was demolished in the 1970s, flooded during the construction of the hydroelectric station on the Dniester River. There used to be people, houses used to line the streets and alleys, gardens blossomed, and the birds sang. The water covered it all.

When I stood many years later on the shore of this reservoir Atlantis, I felt a deep discomfort. It seemed that the life of the place, still vibrant, was deep under the water, that everything had frozen under it, everything that "sang and struggled, / shone brightly and rushed forward," to quote from my favorite Marina Tsvetaeva poem.[25] I sensed that if only the water could be drained, I'd once more see the streets and houses and the people I'd known, and even glimpse among them the youth I'd been.

The newly wed Mikhail and Maya, Stara Ushitsya, Ukraine.

It used to be a small town, Stara Ushitsya, the center of a district in the Khmelnytskyi region. Before the war, it was a shtetl, filled with Jews. It was there, in 1953, as the reader might recall, that I started my career in the district attorney's office. I also learned a story there, which I'm now putting to paper.

This story will be brief, since it is based on the only information I ever got about it. It does not contain the kinds of details that makes such narratives so vivid and real. The people who told it to me—those who were involved in the story itself—did not provide any specifics, and I'm afraid to embellish anything and distort their lived experiences with my imagination. But even if my account were as brief as a telegram, it would still belong on the page. There are stories that simply cannot be forgotten.

My wife, Maya, and I drove to Stara Ushitsya in the back of the truck. The road from Kamyanets-Podilskyi to Stara Ushitsya is a strikingly picturesque fifty-kilometer highway. Its occasional short and flat sections are interspersed with steep climbs, and tight bends, and precipices. Forests often disappear behind high cliffs and from up high can be seen in the abyss. We rode the whole way over this abyss, which took our breath away with its beauty and peril.

Soon after our arrival, we met our neighbors, a married couple, Anya and Pyotr. They were humble and simple people who had three daughters and lived in a tiny house. Anya sold seltzer water in a kiosk and Pyotr worked in the town's sanitation department. We told them how much the road's terrifying beauty had impressed us. They listened to our enraptured impressions, and Anya said: "This road was built by the Jews who were later shot by the Germans. I was there..." Our excitement about the road on the edge of the abyss evaporated, never to return, and gave way to very different feelings.

\*\*\*

Chana lived with her parents in Stara Ushitsya. She finished the ninth grade on the eve of the war. A grade above her at school, there was a boy called Pyotr from the village of Loyivtsi, only seven kilometers away from the district center. Chana and Pyotr couldn't be more dissimilar. The red-headed Chana was the town's beauty. Pyotr was undistinguished in both appearance and height. She was sociable, cheerful, and active. He was a silent brooder and avoided noisy gatherings. Chana was a good student, Pyotr not so much. She loved music and poetry, while he was indifferent to them. Pyotr was in love with Chana; she did not reciprocate his feelings and was apathetic toward him. The young man pined after her, as anyone would, and suffered from his unrequited love.

The Germans arrived in Stara Ushitsya in the first days of the war and began the *aktionen* which they carried out in all of the occupied Soviet territories, the *aktionen* whose consequences still resonate throughout the world many decades after the end of the war.

The whole population was separated into two groups—Jews and non-Jews. The latter could live. In servitude, oppressed, in terror—but they could live. The Jews had to die, disappear from the face of the earth. The borderline between life and death was like a watershed that divided people who just one day earlier had been neighbors visiting each other's homes, working together, studying together, falling in love, marrying each other, and starting families together. The war also intensified old hatreds that had always been under the surface. Pyotr and Chana ended on the opposite sides of the watershed because she was Jewish.

When the war began, the highway between Kamyanets-Podilskyi and Stara Ushitsya was not yet finished. It was important for the Germans as a strategic road, so they decided to use the Jews they'd doomed to death to complete its construction. They set up a ghetto in Kamyanets-Podilskyi and herded into it the Jews from the nearby areas, including from Stara Ushitsya, as well as much farther places, like Hungary. Chana was interned in the ghetto.

Pyotr learned about it when he was back home in his village. He took a small knapsack, put a loaf of bread, a piece of lard, a knife, and a sack in it, and set out without telling anyone. He reached the ghetto by evening and kidnapped Chana from it. He put her into the sack and hoisted it onto his back. Thirty-two kilometers separated the ghetto from his village. He walked all this way along the road above the abyss, the road lined with forests and cliffs, carrying his priceless cargo in the sack, afraid to encounter anyone. He brought Chana home in the dark and freed her from the sack in front of his astonished family members.

Pyotr and his family hid Chana during the entire period of the German occupation. She caught typhus and survived only thanks to their care. Gradually, Chana turned into Anya and became Pyotr's wife.

And that is the whole story. However, now I told it, I need to revisit the question I raised at the beginning—the question of details. The reader, I think, may have a few questions of their own: How did Pyotr manage to kidnap Chana from a ghetto guarded by the Germans? How was it possible to hide Chana in Pyotr's house during the long, horrible years of the occupation? These are certainly reasonable questions, but I cannot answer them, as Anya and Pyotr did not give me these details. And I did not ask.

Anna and Pyotr Gutsol, Stara Ushitsya, Ukraine.

Many in Stara Ushitsya knew this story in the early postwar years. From some I heard a version in which Pyotr paid one of the Ukrainian ghetto guardsmen to get Chana out and later was able to obtain forged documents for her, so she could pass as his relative. Perhaps that is indeed what happened. I'm relaying only what I heard from Chana and Pyotr's mouths: a village boy freed a Jewish girl he loved from a ghetto, carried her in a sack for many kilometers, hid her in his house, and thus saved her.

Was Chana able to fall in love with Pyotr, reciprocate his love, the love which saved her life? Or did feelings of respect and gratitude develop in the place of love? We don't know, and it is not for us to know. When we met them, we saw a faithful wife, a caring mother, and a gracious hostess. And what about

Pyotr? He would always look at his Anna-Chana with the same adoring eyes!

Before Stara Ushitsya was flooded, its residents scattered to wherever they could, running from a sinking ship. Prior to their departure, Pyotr came to Kamyanets-Podilskyi, where I was working at the time, and stopped in to say goodbye. He was leaving with the family for Odesa...

I never saw Anna or Pyotr again. I don't know where they are during these turbulent times. I hope that they're all right, that fate or God smiles upon them and their children... For if they aren't blessed, who will be?[26]

# 17. One Day in the Life of a Detective

A nine-months-long investigation was coming to a close. Its extraordinary duration was due to the nature and magnitude of the criminal case, which involved large-scale embezzlement, bribery, and financial abuses in the construction administration in the town of Shepetivka. One notable construction project in town, which was at the center of the ongoing embezzlement, was the museum dedicated to the life and legacy of Nikolai Ostrovsky, the bedridden author of the socialist realist classic *How the Steel Was Tempered*, a native of Shepetivka. The whole country knew about the museum and its original architectural design, which was partially supported by donations from the inspired townsfolk.

Goldis on the left in Shepetivka, Ukraine.

None of this, however, had any impact on the quality and tempo of the building work. It dragged on and on, as did our investigation. Ten employees in the administration, including its manager, were being held, and ten more were criminally charged. Investigated by a large group of detectives, the case was laborious and there were boxes upon boxes of documents. I was in charge of it on behalf of the region's attorney's office and spent most of my time in Shepetivka. The intensity of our schedule was overwhelming; I barely had any weekends and stopped going back home to Kamyanets-Podilskyi altogether.

The discomfort of being away from home was almost unbearable. In need of a good shower and a wash, I was struck by a simple idea—a bathhouse! Even a godforsaken town like this must have a bathhouse, I thought, and off I headed in search of one. Someone wise once said that a shower at home is only good for washing away one's dirt, but that only in a bathhouse can one truly enjoy the process. Perhaps it's true.

Blissfully clean and half-dressed, I went up to the bathhouse attendant. I needed to resolve one small, but delicate matter with him: I had to wash some of my clothes, but doing laundry was completely prohibited in the bathhouse, as the large signs on walls sternly announced. Having explained to the attendant that I was not from town and was on a protracted business trip, I asked him for a one-time exception to the rules.

The attendant was an elderly man. His reaction to my request was unexpected and bizarre. His face turned crimson and he began to look me up and down in silence, stepping to the side, and then returning to again examine me. It was clear that my request agitated and confused him. I couldn't understand why, but assumed that he was a very conscientious worker. Did my wish for a small favor offend his professionalism?

At last, he uttered: "Are you really asking me about laundry?" I was overjoyed that he had finally said something and quickly blurted out my request again. In response, I heard: "Let me do your laundry for you while you stay here a bit longer in the shower." "What a nutcase," I thought, and politely declined the offer. But he explained to me where and how I could do my laundry—and I got busy.

When I'd finished, got dressed, and was about to leave, the attendant approached me. As I thanked him, he said that he'd like to invite me to his house. He did not live far and had told his wife about me. She was getting ready for their guest. "Please, don't turn down our invitation," he said, and somewhat slyly added, "I didn't refuse your request, did I?" I was just about to politely say no, but I was intrigued and my intuition told me to accept.

I followed this person I hardly knew down the streets of the unfamiliar town. We entered his tiny apartment, where everything indicated that poor and elderly people lived here. They clearly did not have much, but there was some food on the table, which the hostess invited me to try, as is the custom in Ukraine, even in the poorest of households. At supper, we talked about everything, including the war; my gracious host was a veteran like me. The whole time there, I kept trying to work out why he'd invited me. I couldn't ask him directly, but he soon provided the explanation.

He had worked as an attendant in the town's bathhouse for the past twenty years. Not once during those two decades had anyone asked him for a permission to do anything. You weren't allowed to do laundry or drying clothes in, but everyone did. It was forbidden to bring food and alcohol into the bathhouse, but everyone ate and drank to their heart's content there. No one respected his authority; he was simply invisible to everyone. Some drunkards would notice him once in a while and make fun of him or play a dirty trick.

At first, this had bothered and agitated him, but then he got used to everything and just put up with it. However, today, for the first time in many years, someone had addressed him in a professional manner and treated him like a fellow human being. He hadn't believed his eyes and ears at first, and had expected a prank, but nothing like that had happened, and he was overjoyed. And that's it. Walking back to the hotel, I thought about how easy it is to humiliate a person and how little a person needs to feel happy.[27]

On the way to the hotel, I recalled another bathhouse episode which took place when my wife, our then little daughter, and I spent a vacation in Haisyn with my mother-in-law, Polina Aronovna Roiter. She was a person of absolute integrity, a long-suffering woman who'd lost her son and husband at the front. A selfless and devoted mother and grandmother, she'd stoically weathered all the trials and tribulations the fate bestowed upon her. She really was an incredible person.

One day during the vacation, I set out for the bathhouse. After waiting in a long line, I advanced toward the cashier's booth, only to realize that I didn't have any money on me. Irritated, I fumbled through my pockets, but there wasn't a kopeck to be found. Not only did I now have to go back home, but I'd have to come back and wait in line again.

The grey-haired cashier was patiently waiting for my payment, while a few angry voices behind me demanded that I get out of the way. I asked the cashier whether I could leave my clean undershirt with her and bring the money later, but she graciously responded: "Young man, do not worry, there's

Maya and Mikhail with their daughter Tatyana dressed
in a Ukrainian national costume, circa 1959, Krasyliv, Ukraine.

no need to leave anything. Here's a ticket; you can bring the money later, and if you don't..." She stopped without finishing her sentence, looked me in the eyes and smiled.

When I was done, I rushed home from the bathhouse, eager to return my miniscule debt. I grabbed the money without explaining anything to the family and brought it to the cashier, profusely thanking her. I went back home, relieved, and told everyone about my little adventure. "Do you know who that bathhouse cashier is?" Polina Aronovna asked me. And without waiting for my answer, she added: "It's Ushakova."

The Ushakovs were a well-known family in town. He was a hero of civil war, whose Ninth Cavalry Division had been stationed in Haisyn; she was a bright and educated woman, involved in various cultural activities. They were a beautiful couple. But in 1937, everything came to a devastating end:

he was declared an "enemy of the people" and she became one by association. They entered the circles of Stalinist hell.

In the fall of 1940, two former division commanders, both now "enemies of the people," met on the Gulag highway. One of them, Alexander Gorbatov, was about to be transported to Moscow for an appeal while the other, Konstantin Ushakov, was staying put in the camp. By some unheard of miracle, Gorbatov was fully rehabilitated and reinstated in his position. He became a renowned commander during World War II, an army general, and a Hero of the Soviet Union. In his memoirs, Gorbatov described meeting Ushakov in Nakhodka bay on his way to Moscow:

> We heartily embraced . . . Ushakov was not sent to Kolyma because of his health: an old warrior, he was wounded nineteen times while fighting with the insurgents in Central Asia; he was decorated with four orders for his bravery—a rarity at that time . . . On the eve of my departure from the bay, I found Kostya Ushakov in a ditch he was digging. Short, emaciated, and weakened, he sat, resting his head on the shovel. After learning that I'd be leaving tomorrow for Moscow, he asked me to tell them there in Moscow that he was innocent and never was an "enemy of the people." We embraced again and parted forever. Of course, I diligently fulfilled his request and passed it on the best I could. But soon after our meeting, he died."[28]

This is Gorbatov's account, but in Haisyn, the town in which Ushakov was respected and from which he was shipped to servitude and death, branded an "enemy of the people," a legend started to spread. When the war began, it was said, Ushakov wrote a letter to Stalin asking to be sent to the front as a private, so that he could once again defend his motherland and put his military experience to noble use. Sometime later, Ushakov was called in by the camp authorities who informed him that his request had been denied. On the way to the barracks, Ushakov had a heart attack and died.[29]

His wife was arrested and sent to the camp, along with the other spouses of generals and marshals. Having entered the Gulag circle of hell, these women continued to believe in their husbands' innocence and hoped against hope for a miracle. Whenever a warden walked into their barracks, they would line up against the wall holding hands, so that if one of them received any news about her husband, good or bad, she wouldn't drop to the floor unconscious and smash her head on the cold cement. Instead, she'd slowly slide down against the wall.

When I saw Ushakova, sitting behind the cashier's window, her journey through hell was already over. She'd returned from the camp with her husband fully rehabilitated and, therefore, she herself too. She'd returned to the town where they'd both once been esteemed, hoping that her knowledge and experience could be put to good use, as her husband had hoped, when he'd begged to be sent to the front. The town's authorities, however, did not want to do anything risky. Despite the fact that she was rehabilitated, the common wisdom in the country, which lasted for decades, was that "no one was imprisoned for nothing." As a result, authorities could think of nothing else that to offer this traumatized woman a job as a cashier in the bathhouse, which guaranteed that she would remain a pauper until her dying day. We sat and shared these thoughts and stories in my mother-in-law's home after my return from the bathhouse.[30]

And this is what I was also thinking about after my visit to the bathhouse in Shepetivka, where I met the attendant who'd never heard a kind word in his life—not from the authorities and not from anyone he served daily at work . . .

# Notes

1 Mikhail Gol'dis, *Puti-Dorogi. Vospominaniia sledovatelia* (Minneapolis: N.p., 2013).

2 I couldn't have written the family history part of this introduction had my grandmother not left for me a Soviet school notebook which she filled with family history and detailed family trees.

3 Marat Grinberg, *The Soviet Jewish Bookshelf: Jewish Culture and Identity between the Lines* (Waltham: Brandeis University Press, 2023).

4 Marat Grinberg, *"I am to be read not from left to right, but in Jewish: from right to left": The Poetics of Boris Slutsky* (Boston: Academic Studies Press 2013).

5 Soviet republics consisted of regions (*oblasti*), divided into districts (*rayony*). The operating branch belonged to regional executive committee (*oblispolkom*), district executive committee (*rayispolkom*), and municipal committee (*gorispolkom*). In reality, as Goldis makes clear, all the governmental branches were subservient to the Communist Party and its various committees.

6 Most likely this massacre took place after the summer of 1942. The Israeli historian Yitzhak Arad writes in his massive *The Holocaust in the Soviet Union*, trans. Ora Cummings (Jerusalem: Yad Vashem, 2009) "Once the mass murder of Jews was completed and following the April–May 1942 directives that a Jew is anyone who has at least one Jewish parent, there began the systematic murder of Jewish spouses in mixed marriages and their offspring" (366). Arad provides testimonies about the murders of children of mixed marriages from the Ukrainian cities of Zaporizhzhia and Melitopol.

7 At the end of Nikolai Gogol's canonical play, the characters freeze, paralyzed by the news that the real inspector general has arrived in town.

8 This episode is a vivid illustration of both Goldis's philosophy and fascination with religion. Despite the fact that he always retained genuine skepticism about all organized religions, including Jewish observance, he was fascinated with spirituality. In Odesa, he befriended a priest in a monastery, Serafim P. Pokrovsky, and held long conversations with him about his faith. Still in Ukraine, after I started to develop an interest in Judaism as a teenager and voraciously read everything that became available about it during Perestroika, my grandfather was deeply

supportive and questioned me about how Judaism explained the presence of evil in the world, divine justice, and divine silence. When he died, it was hard to find a rabbi who could officiate at his funeral in person because it was still during the pandemic. Knowing how he always preferred the personal over the formal, I conducted the funeral myself in both Hebrew and Russian.

9   In 1996, unbeknownst to Goldis, Khoma Matsyuk was recognized as Righteous Among the Nations by Yad Vashem; and in 2000, his daughter received the same honor. See "Matsiuk Homa & Natalia ; Daughter: Ukrainetz Solomiya (Matsiuk), Yadvashem.org, accessed November 26, 2023, https://righteous.yadvashem.org/?searchType=righteous_only&language=en&itemId=4035689&ind=0. There are a few discrepancies between Kats's testimony here and the account presented to Yad Vashem. One significant detail is that the Katses' two daughters were murdered in 1941 while the parents were on a forced labor excursion from the ghetto. There are also a number of other memoirs and documents which confirm that Kats was a witness in trials of collaborators after the war. One puzzling detail which I was unable to unlock is that while Kats's name is Meir here, in other sources he's referred to as Moisei or Moish. Perhaps his official name was Meir. Overall, this chapter is a rare and vivid example of how Holocaust memory was formed and transmitted among Jews in the Soviet Union. Unlike in other cases (see, for instance, the chapter "The Road above the Abyss"), Kats is not afraid to discuss the role of collaborators. It's also telling that he primarily sees in Goldis a fellow Jew he can trust rather than a representative of the regime. Goldis's voice and demeanor are distinctly different here than in the criminal cases. If in the latter, he is inquisitive, wants to fill in all the details, and owns the narrative, so to speak, here he's a silent chronicler and a listener.

10  Oleksiy Vatchenko (1914-1984) served as the first secretary of the Communist Party Committee of the Khmelnitskyi Region from 1959-1963. By all accounts, he was the worst kind of party apparatchik. He is also infamous in the history of Soviet Ukrainian literature. Oles Honchar, a major Soviet Ukrainian writer, provided a veiled, but scathing portrait of him in his novel *Sobor* (The Cathedral), written in 1968. Vatchenko recognized himself in the character and demanded that the novel be destroyed, which is what happened.

11  Goldis was a big fan of this series which was based on the novel by the brothers Vainer and depicted the criminal mayhem of the early postwar years. He was particularly taken with the character of Zhiglov, an unconventional and at times ruthless detective, especially because he

was played by Vladimir Vysotsky (1938-1980), a cult actor and singer, many of whose songs were Goldis's favorites.

12   Nikolai Lyashenko served in this position from 1959-1980. Goldis had a difficult relationship with him, especially toward the end of Lyashenko's career.

13   This is one of the central episodes in memoir, as it provides not only a window into antisemitism in Soviet Ukraine, but also into Goldis's character. I often asked him why, after being exposed to such open discrimination and hate, he didn't resign, or become a dissident, or try to emigrate. He explained that while he decided to stay on partly because he felt that he could continue to do good, the main reason was that he couldn't jeopardize his family. Emigration was not a viable option at that point, in other words. It is episodes like these, however, that strengthened his Jewish identity. The following lines from one of Boris Slutsky's sardonic poems describe Goldis's attitude well: "I love the antisemites / who for free give me their lessons / point to me my faults / and appoint the deadlines / which are supposed to drive me mad."

14   On *The Commissar* and the city, see my study of the film. Marat Grinberg, *Alexander Askoldov: The Commissar* (Bristol: Intellect, 2016).

15   Bernard Lewis writes in his seminal *Semites and Anti-Semites*, "Embezzlement, theft, bribery, currency speculation, and corruption in general have long plagued the Soviet Union. From time to time the Soviet authorities launched campaigns against such crimes. . . . A major campaign of this kind was conducted between 1961 and 1964, in which Jews were singled out as the main victims . . . of eighty-four persons sentenced to death for economic crimes in 1962, forty-five were Jews, i.e. 54 percent. In the Ukrainian Republic the proportion was seventeen out of twenty-one, or 81 percent." Bernard Lewis, *Semites and Anti-Semites* (W. W. Norton & Company 1987), 40.

16   Grigory Andreevich Tonkocheev (1904-1991) was the mayor of Kamyanets-Podilskyi from 1953-1968. The city developed tremendously during his tenure. An avid soccer fan, he built a large stadium. Tonkocheev was Goldis's neighbor in the building on the street Leningradskaya 50 (now Lesya Ukrainka) where Goldis lived with his family from 1962-1969. The building now bears a plaque in honor of Tonkocheev.

17   The defense attorney Fillip Yakovlevich Kramer was Goldis's close friend. He emigrated with his family to the US in the early 1990s and died in Philadelphia ten years ago.

18  The judge was Anatoly Vasilievich Mitskevich. My mother, Tatyana, was named after Mitskevich's wife.

19  A traditional Klezmer melody, the lyrics to which were composed by Rudolf Fuchs in the 1970s, there's indeed no definitive explanation for why this dance is called "Seven Forty." According to one urban legend, it refers to the train which brought people to Odesa from the nearby towns, arriving at 7:40 a.m. For more information on the song/dance and various theories about its name, see Boris Dralyuk, "Herzl in Odessa. Not at 7:40 . . . ," Boris Dralyuk: Essays, Translations, and Other Writings, October 2, 2020, https://bdralyuk.wordpress.com/2020/10/02/herzl-in-odessa-not-at-740/.

20  Nikolai Rozbam died in 2020. His widow and son, also Nikolai, with his family continue to reside in Kamyanets-Podilskyi. I shared this chapter with Nikolai Rozbam Jr. and he was heartened to discover that his father's actions and memory would live on.

21  This first section of the chapter is one of the strongest in the entire memoir from an aesthetic standpoint and reveals what a truly talented writer Goldis was. The phantasmagoric atmosphere and the unconscious stroll through the wintery ancient town is reminiscent of Kafka, particularly, his short story "The Country Doctor." Goldis discovered Kafka in the late 1990s, when I became an avid reader and researcher of his work, and read him with fascination.

22  The name Valya-Valentina also brings to mind a canonical Soviet poem by Eduard Bagritsky (1895-1934) "The Death of a Young Pioneer Girl," well-known to Goldis. The poem describes a young Communist, Valya-Valentina, dying from tuberculosis, who refuses to succumb to her mother's pleas and put on a cross. For a discussion of Bagritsky's poetry, see Maxim D. Shrayer, *Russian Poet/Soviet Jew: The Legacy of Eduard Bagritskii* (New York: Rowman & Littlefield, 2000). Goldis's description of her character as "beautiful and morally upright" is also tongue-in-cheek and invokes a classic Soviet film comedy *Prisoner of the Caucasus or Shurik's New Adventures* (1967), in which the main female character (Natalya Varlei), abducted to be married, is described precisely in this manner. Like the film, Goldis ridicules the Soviet language.

23  This sentence encapsulates Goldis's judicial and moral philosophy. On abortions in the Soviet Union, see Michele Rivkin-Fish, *Unmasking Russia's Abortion Culture: Family Planning and the Struggle for a Liberal Biopolitics* (Nashville: Vanderbilt University Press, forthcoming June 15, 2024).

24 My grandfather, his sister Nella, and I visited my great-grandfather's resting place before we left for the US in the summer of 1993. I brought with me a Jewish calendar, published by the Moscow synagogue, which contained the Mourners' Kaddish. I recited the Kaddish for my great-grandfather there.

25 One of Russia's greatest twentieth-century poets, Marina Tsvetaeva (1892-1941) was among Goldis's favorites, so much so that he even wrote an essay about her love for Jews and their destiny in the world. The lines he cites come from Tsvetaeva's early poem "Requiem."

26 As in the case with "Meir and Khoma," unbeknownst to Godlis, Pyotr Gutsol (1922-2005) was declared a Righteous Among the Nations by Yad Vashem in 1994. The account, provided by Yad Vashem, fills in some of the details he and Anna (maiden name Birman) didn't tell my grandparents, many of them riveting and touching on the deadly collaboration of the local population. The most moving detail of Pyotr's love for Anna, the very reason he saved her, is not, however, in the Yad Vashem version. As to why it was not revealed, one can only guess. This poignant and beautiful short chapter is a testimony to how Holocaust memory—fragmentary, cautious, and yet powerful—existed in the Soviet Union. Considering the devastation brought to Ukraine today by Russia's aggression, which undoubtedly is impacting Pyotr and Anna's children and grandchildren and perhaps Anna herself if she's still alive, throws a deeply tragic light on Goldis's last sentence, "For if they aren't blessed, who will be?" See "Gutzol Peotr," Yadvashem.org, accessed November 26, 2023. https://collections.yadvashem.org/en/righteous/4015161.

27 This episode again reveals Goldis's talent as a writer. The portrait of the bath attendant is an homage to a host of "little people" in the nineteenth-century Russian literary canon, the lowly and humiliated civil servants who call to be treated with dignity and count on their oppressors' shared humanity.

28 Goldis is quoting from Aleksandr Gorbatov, *Gody i voiny. Zapiski komandarma 1941-1945* (Moscow: Tsentrpoligraf 2008), 250-251.

29 Goldis is right to frame this as a legend. Ushakov indeed pleaded with the government to allow him to return to the front. His request was finally granted in 1943, but he died soon after from pellagra in the camp. He was fully rehabilitated in 1957.

30 The account of Ushakov's wife's journey is largely accurate here. Anna Yulievna Ushakova was arrested on March 10, 1938 and sentenced to eight years of hard labor for spying. She was sent to the Karaganda

camp. She returned to Haysin after the war, worked in the bathhouse, and, according to one account, died from a psychiatric illness. See "Vospominaniia o bylom," Memoirs.memo.ru, accessed November 26, 2023, https://memoirs.memo.ru/memoir/show/id/202 and Nikolai Cherushev, *Iz Gulaga—v boi* (Moscow: Veche 2013), 113.

www.ingramcontent.com/pod-product-compliance
Lightning Source LLC
Chambersburg PA
CBHW021157160426
43194CB00007B/775